Dyslexia and Information and Communications Technology

Dyslexia and Information and Communications Technology

A Guide for teachers and parents

2nd edition

ANITA KEATES

David Fulton Publishers
London

David Fulton Publishers Ltd
The Chiswick Centre, 414 Chiswick High Road, London W4 5TF
www.fultonpublishers.co.uk

First published in Great Britain in 2000 by David Fulton Publishers

Note: The rights of Anita Keates to be identified as the author of this work have been asserted by her in accordance with the Copyright, Designs and Patents Act 1988.

David Fulton Publishers is a division of Granada Learning Limited, part of Granada plc.

British Library Cataloguing in Publication Data
A catalogue record for this book is available from the British Library.

ISBN 1-85346-757-X

Typeset by FiSH Books, London

Contents

This book is dedicated to
my two sons
Robin and Simeon

and

Yorick their Labrador dog

Acknowledgements

I would like to thank the following:

my family for their help;
Dr C. Singleton;
Father Alan Cotgrove of the BDACC; and
the pupils, staff and parents of the schools.

Reviews

Good reasons for recommending this book. Its narrative style is relaxed and easy for computer phobic teachers or parents of dyslexic children. When technical details are necessary, they are explained and placed in context. It has many real examples of children's responses and work to illustrate teaching and learning points.

Judith Stansfield (2000) *Computers and Education*

Anita Keates' useful guide to information and communications technology issues and resources goes beyond an instantly out-of-date software listing, to discuss educational paths from the point of view of dyslexic children and their families and teachers. This serves both as a reassuring introduction and realistic guide to what technology will (and will not) achieve.

The Times Educational Supplement

Dyslexia and Information and Communcations Technology: superbly designed, full of information on hardware and software; it shows how ICT can be utilised to enhance the literacy skills of dyslexic children. *Dyslexia and Information and Communcations Technology* does guide the reader through the quagmire of terms and resources in ICT and shows how these can benefit dyslexic learners.

Lannen, S. and Lannen, C. (December 2000) *British Journal of Special Education*, **27**(4)

Anita Keates, however, has managed to produce a very readable and useful text in an area of ICT that should become an essential addition to the bookshelves of teachers and parents alike.

Reviewed by Victoria Crivelli, Senior Specialist Teacher ICT and Resources Learning Support Service, Worcester, UK in *Child Language Teaching and Therapy*

As the title suggests, this is a book written to promote and facilitate the use of ICT with dyslexic students. The book is a 'family concern' written by a mother of a dyslexic with the foreword provided by a brother. The foreword is a good 'thumbnail sketch' of the plight of a truly dyslexic child from a very personal viewpoint and as such conveys powerfully and effectively the nature of the difficulty. This would be a good piece for those, especially among the teaching profession, who remain stubbornly sceptical as to whether dyslexia even exists and who, at times, continue to cause dyslexic children and adults distress.

The book is based on a personal journey of the experience of the author as she seeks to effectively help her son and early on discovers the releasing power of ICT for dyslexic children. The text is clear and well written in a relatively jargon free 'user friendly' style that doesn't alienate or distance the reader. The content is well organised and successfully categorises and evaluates the different aspects of ICT hardware and software that can be used with dyslexic students. The summaries at the end of each chapter are useful and informative. Being based on personal experience it does at times verge on the over opinionated, i.e. 'this works and this doesn't'. In the same way, the text can be a little subjective, for example, I don't feel it necessary for the reader to know which icon in a particular word processing facility is the authoresses favourite! (p. 52).

This is a particularly good resource for parents who want to get the right ICT equipment for their child and can afford what is available. They are often faced with a whole range of expensive ICT hardware and software without any information as to their effectiveness in a situation where it is tempting to grab anything that suggests the possibility of bringing relief to the child's distress. For a teacher dealing with dyslexic pupils, it is a bit like going on a good course where you'd like to use lots of the equipment practically, if only finances would permit. The book provides a useful, detailed reference point for information about the best ICT available for pupils with Specific Learning Difficulties.

The authoress achieves her objectives of showing that when appropriately used, ICT can be a powerful releasing 'tool' for dyslexics and can certainly make life easier. It is also a useful guide for purchasing ICT in this context, being lent credibility by the fact that the author is chairperson of the British Dyslexic Association's computer committee and is therefore likely to have the most up-to-date and relevant information for parent and teacher alike. It should certainly facilitate informed choice when seeking to use ICT with dyslexics and help to avoid the pitfall of spending money badly under pressure when seeking to bring relief to a dyslexic child or adult.

K. Green, teacher of dyslexic students, OLCHS, Lancaster.
Journal of Computer Assisted Learning (2001) **17**, 221–2

Foreword

One of my earliest memories is of my brother, Robin, running incessantly round the garden, screaming at the top of his voice. Over the years this became fairly typical behaviour for him and was something of an enigma to me, a child three years his junior. Later, when I was old enough to understand such things, it was clear that he was full of anger and embitterment which he was incapable of expressing to anyone else. Without the usual outlet of calming down by talking with someone, the only method of alleviating his frustration available to him was complete physical exhaustion.

Numerous educational professionals failed to explain how a child with his high IQ could be labelled by his teachers as educationally subnormal. Several teachers used derogatory terms such as 'thick', 'lazy' or 'slow' and despite the confirmed evidence from educational psychologists about his IQ, they were only willing to accept the results of their own written tests, tests that Robin often performed very badly in.

Consequently, he was placed in classes with children far below his level of intelligence and given tasks to perform that were the educational equivalent of basket-making. Teachers simply tried to find activities that were aimed primarily at keeping him occupied and educational value was of only secondary importance.

Robin's reasons for disenchantment with his life at school were obvious and the effects of this began to spill over into other areas of his life. In the desperation typical of the parents of a child who was not behaving in accordance with their hopes or expectations, my parents took him to yet another psychologist. After another afternoon of questioning and intelligence tests, he was finally diagnosed as dyslexic.

Although at the time the definition of dyslexia was accepted as 'word blindness', it was a watershed in terms of understanding why Robin behaved in the way that he did.

Think about the importance of being able to process the written word. It should not be underestimated. Books are one of the most common media for the storage of knowledge. You are probably reading this one in the hope of gaining information and new insights. Many accepted cultural modes of behaviour are defined in books or newspapers. Whole worlds of different views, opinions and experiences are contained in the numerous pages in any library. These worlds, those experiences, are inaccessible to those who cannot read text on a page – those that often need them the most.

With an impaired ability to process the written word, typical dyslexics have no method of understanding what accepted behaviour is without going though a very painful period of personal trial and error. Nor can they gain rapidly the emotional maturity needed to express their feelings. Robin had neither the vocabulary nor the semantic reasoning to explain, or even understand, what he was feeling.

However, from Robin's perspective, these were minor issues when compared to the difficulties presented by the educational establishment. The methods of teaching that he encountered invariably focused on the imparting of knowledge through the written word, often on a blackboard, and the assessment of how well that knowledge had been processed by written exams.

For Robin, with his impaired ability to read, the lessons were obviously very difficult and often painful. Even armed with the understanding of the basic symptoms of his dyslexia, his more sympathetic teachers still struggled to find methods of providing the information in a format that he could understand. The others flatly refused to acknowledge the very existence of dyslexia and continued to persecute him, as he saw it, for his lack of achievement. Exam results were always a deeply unpleasant time of year, with teachers often showing no mercy with their comments. My parents continued to despair of Robin ever getting the official recognition that his talent deserved.

And then something miraculous happened.

One Christmas, my parents decided to buy a joint present for Robin and me – something bigger and more expensive than we would normally get. It was a Dragon 32 microcomputer. Compared to today's powerful computers this was almost laughably under-whelming. The 32 kilobytes of memory are a fraction of the basic unit of memory on a modern PC. It supported eight colours on a television screen, loaded programs through a standard tape recorder and the keyboard did not even have lower case letters.

But the effect on Robin was amazing.

Being children, our first response was to try out the games that had been bundled with the computer. One was a text-based adventure that Robin quickly consigned to the bottom of the box, but the other was an adventure game with a very simple yet effective graphical interface. Here was something with which he could interact without the use of long sentences or the fear of being assessed or judged.

Hours passed by while Robin moved a block around a screen, fighting groups of ogres, bartering in markets and eventually defeating the evil lord in his citadel. Robin adored it.

He did not care that he was learning how many swords at 60 gold pieces he could buy with his bag of 300 pieces; nor that complicated planning was required to marshal his forces by the most direct route through the swamps and mountain passes to minimise troop losses. What mattered was that he was achieving success for possibly the first time that he could remember.

As the weeks passed by, the time taken for him to defeat the evil lord was becoming significantly shorter, and I soon found out why. Robin had discovered that if he tried to sell his gold pieces to the trader for two pieces each the trader would refuse, but if he then followed it up with a request for 1.99 pieces, the trader would accept. Consequently, he could virtually double his money whenever he chose and keep doing so, a brilliant feat of lateral thinking – one step better than the programmer at least!

My parents noticed Robin's enthusiasm for playing with the computer and began to nurture it. As the power of computers developed, they encouraged him to use increasingly sophisticated software, such as word-processors and spreadsheets. My mother realised that if the content of his school lessons could be translated onto the computer, then perhaps Robin would begin to lose his fear of school. As a result of this early foray into the use of computers, Robin now holds two degrees and has a successful career as an engineering consultant.

The purpose of recounting this episode is to show the power of involving information technology in assisting those with dyslexia, not only in meeting educational goals, but in personal development as well. This book builds on the lessons learned with Robin and numerous other dyslexic students. They have all benefited from the use of technology in moving the classroom from a place of rigid stricture to a stimulating, multisensory and multimodal forum for the exchange of information. The aim is to encourage the reader to think about methods of teaching in their broadest sense, to look beyond the confines of copying notes from blackboards and not to shy away from technology.

With the rise of the Internet, more powerful methods of storing information and faster computers to process it, there are new worlds of wonder to experience in formats that allow dyslexics to access them.

Help them to do so: the rewards are remarkable.

Dr Simeon Keates, MA (Cantab), PhD (Cantab)

Introduction

In the course of researching this book I have tried to find a single agreed definition of dyslexia. However, after discovering over 28 different ones and not even exhausting my search, I gave up. An example definition from the Orton Dyslexia Society (1995) is as follows:

> Dyslexia is a neurologically based, often familial, disorder, which inter-feres with the acquisition and processing of language. Varying in degrees of severity, it is manifested by difficulties in receptive and expressive language, including phonological processing, in reading, writing, spelling, handwriting and sometimes in arithmetic.

As one would expect from such a large number of definitions, information regarding the actual constituents of dyslexia varies greatly. The most common consensus though, is that the reading and spelling ability of the dyslexic student is not, for whatever reason, commensurate with his or her intelligence. The impact of this disadvantage becomes apparent when one looks at the following quotation from the School Curriculum Assessment Authority (1995) and although it expressly refers to reading, it is equally pertinent to writing skills:

> *The consequences of reading problems for children's learning*
> The negative consequences of reading problems are likely to increase with time. Early reading problems can initiate a causal chain of effects. Very quickly, poorer readers encounter less text than their peers. By the time children reach the middle primary years it has been estimated that the least motivated children might read 100,000 words a year, while the average reader might encounter 1,000,000 words of text. The more voracious readers might read as many as 10,000,000 words. The situation is exacerbated by the fact that poorer readers are often given books to read that are too difficult for them. As word reading skill develops, more general language skills become the limiting factor on reading ability. But the greater reading experience of the better reader has provided an enormous advantage even here.

As stated in the Orton Dyslexia Society (1995) definition of dyslexia, there are varying degrees of severity and one must also bear in mind that nurture will have played a part. However, dyslexia itself goes much deeper than this, and reading, writing and spelling difficulties are mere symptoms.

Nevertheless, to be so many million words behind at the age of 7 has a considerable impact and this situation becomes compounded as pupils get older, unless positive steps are taken to counter it. It is at this stage that any parent begins to panic and become extremely concerned about their apparently disadvantaged child. I do empathise with them.

However, there are also many advantages in being dyslexic, which are only just being researched and one must look to very famous people who are now deemed to be dyslexic. Such disadvantaged people include Albert Einstein, Leonardo da Vinci and Sir Winston Churchill. As a parent and teacher, I personally found that once I understood the way a dyslexic child operated and thought, then I could deal better with the situation and teach appropriately.

What is Information and Communications Technology (ICT)?

ICT, the use of computers in education, used to be known simply as Information Technology (IT). IT was at first principally focused on programming where the pupil was taught a programming language and wrote programs to solve specific, usually artificial, problems. Software was very expensive and it was often easier to write your own program. This is not the case now. Programming has become a very specialist skill and computer usage is now much broader than that. It became apparent that the technology was advancing and consequently the skills that were needed were changing.

While this change in computer usage was occurring, the National Curriculum (NC) was being introduced into the schools of England and Wales for ten subjects, one of which was IT. I was fortunate enough to be an advisory teacher for IT and special educational needs (SEN) and had a rather talented and knowledgeable adviser who trained me, along with twelve others, in IT and the NC.

IT was designed to be delivered via all NC subjects and, in order to ensure that this was done, IT was specifically mentioned within the individual subject orders. Therefore, when English teachers were teaching their subject, they were required to include IT as a natural part of it. The same applied to science, geography and so on.

The government, however, apparently felt that if IT was not also a subject in its own right, without legislation to ensure its survival, it might be neglected in the curriculum and therefore the NC for IT was written as a separate section. Unfortunately, this separate subject was placed, for whatever reason, in the subject of technology. My role as an advisory teacher was to go to schools to remind them that IT was not part of technology alone, and to encourage teachers of all subjects to include it within their particular subject if it was appropriate. I also had to try to ensure that IT was not taught as a subject isolated from other subjects, which was often the case, particularly in secondary schools.

As a result of this background, I was in a position to understand how useful IT was in every curriculum subject. When the NC was later revised, many subject orders were altered and changed. IT became known as ICT but essentially the NC orders for IT/ICT did not change significantly, with the original ethos still pertaining. It also became apparent that, due to the increasing ubiquity of the computer, ICT was important for all. ICT is an extremely powerful tool that enables people who use computers to do wonderful things. This powerful and flexible tool is useful in schools.

Dyslexic pupils need access to ICT

Dyslexic pupils are often taught by paper systems, which some pupils deem to be demeaning, particularly as they appear to dwell on the negative aspects of being dyslexic, namely spelling and reading. These systems have varying degrees of success but rarely appear to address the immediate problems facing the dyslexic student in a school environment, which is access to the curriculum.

The difficulties facing the pupil in school are essentially as follows.

1. The processing of sound in lessons is a huge problem for most dyslexic students. This results in the student being:

    (a) unable to follow the content of the lesson as well as other students do;
    (b) unable to précis the content for note-taking;
    (c) unable to process homework assignment titles and dates.

2. Note-taking is a considerable problem for most dyslexic students. This causes problems for:

    (a) speed of writing which results in the student omitting words or writing in a way that is not very legible;
    (b) being unable to read what they are writing – which causes the student to lose track of what they are doing – and also being unable to process what is being said.

3. Even if the above two are attempted, the dyslexic student still cannot read at a later date what has been written. This results in further difficulties such as:

    (a) being unable to read homework tasks along with dates for handing in work;
    (b) being unable to access some examination assignments due to being unable to read the task and the notes to support the assignment;
    (c) being unable to use notes for revision purposes.

These difficulties can vary according to the subjects, but even a subject like physical education (PE) now has a written examination paper. While such problems are considerable for secondary school pupils, they are just as pertinent and cause many difficulties to pupils from Key Stage (KS) 1 (infant school, 5–7 years) and KS2 (junior school, 7–11 years). It is also at this younger age that many of the difficulties result in pupils' developing low self-confidence and low self-esteem, for they cannot demonstrate on paper how capable they are. Their potential cannot be expressed in written format, nor can they often read at a level commensurate with their intelligence.

Using ICT can give the pupil access to the curriculum and provide an interesting and creative learning environment, which is ideally suited to the dyslexic student of all ages. It is for this reason that I have written this book. It is intended as a guide for those involved with dyslexic students, such as the parents and teachers of dyslexic children along with dyslexic individuals themselves. Although it primarily covers the usage of ICT from 4 to 16 years, it is also suitable for older students and adults. It is written to provide a stimulus to encourage people to view ICT software in a broader light and in a supportive, rather than confrontational, manner. The aim is to encourage dyslexic students in their studies and to empower them to have a greater control over their learning process and outcomes. I will include specific examples of how ICT can be used in either the classroom or home environment. These are meant as suggestions to stimulate ideas and can be adapted for the individual dyslexic student.

I would like to make it clear that the book is not designed to be a research document, nor a document about the nature of dyslexia. Instead, it is a practical approach, for dyslexic individuals and those who deal with them, about how to use ICT to gain access to the National Curriculum in schools and, by doing so, to deliver ICT NC capability. The result is that the pupils are able to achieve their potential by working at a level commensurate with their intelligence. The practices mentioned are proven methods of working, developed over a number of years, and result in considerable progress being made by the pupils, with an associated improvement in self-confidence and self-esteem.

This book is aimed equally at both parents and teachers and I will attempt to do away with some of the unnecessary mystique that surrounds both dyslexia and ICT. Above all, ICT should be fun and empowering for the student. If used in this way, significant educational strides, with concomitant improvement in behaviour, will result.

For instance, one pupil aged 14 years, who I will call Samantha, began working with me a little over 18 months ago. She had a Statement for Specific Learning Difficulties (Dyslexia), a reading age equivalent to 8.9 years with a quotient of below 70 and average intelligence. Essentially this meant that Samantha was functioning at a level of an average 8- to 9-year-old in reading, which was approximately five years behind her potential. Samantha had some difficulty with her behaviour in that her frustration would quickly surface and she would erupt, with chairs being thrown about, abusive language being used towards the teacher and doors being slammed.

After one year of Samantha working with me, using ICT as an integral part of the lessons, she no longer needed a Statement. Samantha's reading had improved considerably with her making 3$\frac{1}{2}$ years' progress. Improvements have continued and she now has a reading age equivalent to her chronological age and needs very little support other than with a few study skills.

The pupils in the school are in sets according to ability and achievement. Samantha has moved out of the lowest set, where she was placed, and has gained promotion twice so that she is now in a middle-band set where she can better achieve her potential. Samantha should continue to make progress and should access all of her GCSE examinations. Her teachers have already begun revising their estimates of her anticipated grades, with her now being forecast at Grade C in five subjects. We have two years to work with Samantha to achieve this, but I see no reason why this should not happen. Samantha's behaviour has also improved considerably and she has recently been made a school prefect. Samantha uses a laptop computer to access her NC subjects.

Who am I?

I am the mother of two sons and I worked as an English teacher. One of my sons was allergic to books and was struggling to read. He showed all the frustrations and unhappiness typical of a dyslexic pupil. I was informed by the head of the primary school he attended that he was not very bright. The same son, labelled as an educational failure, now has a BSc (Hons) and MSc in Engineering, the latter from Cranfield University.

The knowledge I gained from being a parent, struggling against the system and discovering ICT, while also being an English teacher, placed me in an interesting position. My learning curve was vertical! This increased knowledge resulted in my being promoted to head of a special educational needs department, while still being a member of an English department in an inner-city comprehensive school. During this time I used various paper-based systems for teaching both my son and my pupils.

As a result of purchasing a computer at home, I soon began using computers to assist my pupils in school. These were BBC computers and BBC Masters, which were 32K and 64K machines. Essentially this means they were very basic and not very powerful by modern standards. However, this use of computers quickly resulted in improved examination results for my pupils, which resulted in my obtaining more computers.

I was promoted to the position of Advisory Teacher for IT and SEN and was further promoted to Head of Hummec, which was the IT Centre for Humberside schools. This centre was the ICT centre for training, consultancy and advice for matters relating to ICT across all aspects of the curriculum.

I am now an independent educational consultant and currently work in Foxhills School, Technology College, for pupils aged 11–16 from Monday to Friday. Foxhills School is located on the outskirts of Scunthorpe, North Lincolnshire. On Saturdays I work in St Hughs, an independent school for pupils aged 4–13. St Hughs is in Woodhall Spa in rural Lincolnshire. I currently chair the British Dyslexia Association (BDA) computer committee, hold a post-graduate diploma for Specific Learning Difficulties (Dyslexia), have various other qualifications and travel throughout the United Kingdom and abroad, delivering seminars and lectures.

When the Special Educational Needs Report of the Committee of Enquiry into the Education of Handicapped Children and Young People, was written in May 1978, Baroness Warnock informed a group of us that she had been instructed not to mention dyslexia. Dyslexia remained a dirty word and many teachers and local education authorities (LEAs) refused to accept that it existed. They believed it was an excuse for laziness or something that parents claimed when they could not accept that their child was thick. Slowly the position has changed, although some professionals still debate the existence of dyslexia.

However, in spite of the increased awareness, few people have the expertise to know how best to use the power and flexibility of ICT to support dyslexic pupils. The BDA has a computer committee (BDACC) which has helped to pioneer the role of ICT and dyslexia. No other organisation rivals this committee for its unique knowledge and wealth of expertise. Various members of the computer committee have contributed to aspects in this book and I have denoted this with the letters BDACC alongside their names.

This book is based on my own personal experience and ideas. It is an attempt to provide a creative experience and, therefore, the aim is to stimulate and promote discussion. There is no intention to criticise, even inadvertently, any specific organisations or schemes of work.

Summary

Essentially, ICT helps the dyslexic pupil:

- achieve more of their potential;
- access NC subjects; and
- increase self-esteem and confidence.

Chapter 1

Why Information and Communications Technology?

I used ICT as long ago as 1986 with three pupils. They were aged 13 and the head of English felt that they would have possibly managed a Grade D or maybe C in the GCE (General Certificate in Education) examination which has now become GCSE (General Certificate in Secondary Education).

The head of the school had asked me to justify having BBC computers in my classroom for teaching English and not using them to teach programming skills in the computer room. We both agreed that examination results should be the measure of success. Although this should not be the only judge of success, in this case it was an easily measured and independent criterion. After working with word-processing and a few other basic programs for a period of about 18 months, I entered the three pupils for their GCE exam in English a year early, in the fourth year, equivalent to Y10. The girl gained a Grade A and both of the boys Grade B. Even I was amazed at their success and this resulted in a more generous allocation of computers. This experience, coupled with that of my own son Robin, resulted in the power and uses of ICT becoming apparent to me.

Academic achievement should not be the only measurement of success: the well-being and happiness of the pupils is of paramount importance. My son explained to me, as he grew older, what school life was like for him. Since then, I have encouraged pupils to talk regularly to me about how they feel. It helps for them to know that someone in school understands their frustrations.

Figures 1.1 and 1.2 demonstrate the feelings of two dyslexic pupils. Both pupils were aged 11 years and were Y6.

The pupil who wrote the poem in Figure 1.1 told me that the sad faces represented how he felt people actually saw him. The moon faces are how that pupil demonstrated what he felt he was really like, being so different from his peers.

The pupil who created Figure 1.2 included an ABC book, although he was Y6. This was to represent how unhappy he was at doing what he considered to be baby work. He felt very strongly about this and added that he considered he was being punished by having to do extra work at night. He said that he could not spend much time enjoying himself, like his friends, but had to be constantly reminded of his difficulties by receiving extra tuition.

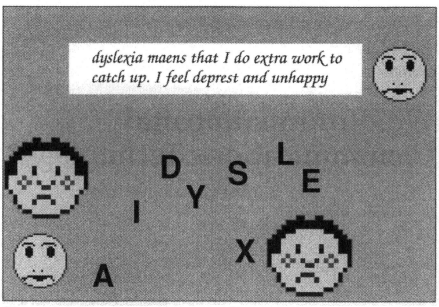

Figure 1.1 Oliver's poem

I also noted that these pupils placed various letters chaotically all over the poems and I asked why this was the case. The one pupil told me it was because he saw letters like that, floating about. The other pupil nodded in agreement. I went home and mentioned this to my son and asked him if he saw letters in words move about while he was trying to read them. He promptly replied, 'Of course. Didn't you know that?'

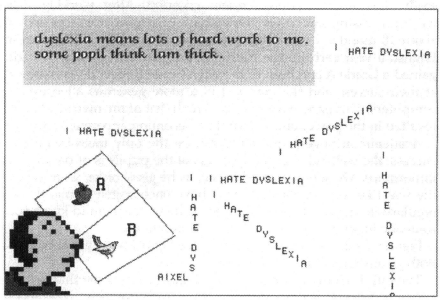

Figure 1.2 David's poem

Dyslexic pupils typically feel that they must be stupid to be given the type of work they are often asked to do. This results in their having low self-confidence and sometimes in their behaviour becoming somewhat challenging. They are often unhappy and deal with their situation in their own way, which can include being switched off to literacy, becoming disruptive and so on.

For these pupils, ICT often represents an environment that they have not failed in. Providing it is used well, ICT is creative. It supports and facilitates their educational development. Using a computer will not graffiti their work with red marks, it will not tell them off or be judgemental. On the contrary it can be exciting and interesting. ICT supports the entire process of writing, by supporting the individual skills involved in that process. Above all, using ICT places the student in greater control.

Most dyslexic pupils are faced with the difficult task of trying to prove how good they are at a subject by being graded on how well they can write about it. This, in turn, is often based on how well they can read the exam questions. Currently I work with a pupil, Bill, who is in Y11. He is the captain for his house and a talented young athlete who has won many cups and medals for his athletic abilities. He captains a football team and loves sport in all of its forms. However, he will have to face either a long or short paper for his GCSE physical education examination, a paper that he will struggle to read and struggle even more to provide written answers for. This means that his final grade could be very low, due to his dyslexia, yet Bill knows the answers to the questions and he definitely has the physical ability and talent for the subject.

Currently, in Foxhills School, Technology College, pupils with dyslexia are gaining access to the exam structure and passing examinations with the help of ICT facilities. As a result of that access, they leave with better employment expectations, or increased prospects in higher or further education. ICT makes a huge difference.

When one adds to this that considerable progress can be made in the pupils' individual reading and writing abilities, along with their thinking and study skills, the overall advantages of ICT become apparent.

How ICT is used for the benefit of dyslexic students

ICT gives access to the curriculum of the subject being taught. NC is an entitlement for all pupils in England and Wales. It has meant a return to basics approach to education requiring an even greater conformity in the provision of education. The content of the curriculum for the pupils in this country is legislated for, and has to be taught and assessed. The NC is divided into four key stages, beginning with KS1, for pupils aged between 5 and 7 years; KS2, 7–11 years; KS3, 11–14 years; and KS4, 14–16 years. In essence, the NC means an entitlement for all pupils to have access to, and be taught, a pre-determined curriculum, stipulated by legislation.

However, it is known that dyslexic pupils find accessing the curriculum particularly difficult, owing to their cluttered short-term memory, phonological processing deficits and so on. As any experienced teacher knows, pupils who feel left out for whatever reason generally become frustrated and disenchanted, which in turn often leads to their being motivationally challenged. While dyslexic pupils are receiving the specified exposure to the National Curriculum subjects, they are not achieving the same progress as other pupils. It can, therefore, be argued that NC provision is meeting the letter, but not the spirit, of the law. To rectify this, it is necessary to look beyond traditional learning techniques and embrace more accessible teaching environments.

By focusing on the specific educational needs of the dyslexic pupil, with a little creative thought, it is possible to make significant improvements using existing mainstream software applications normally used to deliver ICT NC capability and entitlement. This aspect of ICT is far more important than looking at specific software as a panacea, although some specific software will be discussed in Chapter 10.

ICT capability

It is necessary at this stage to mention ICT capability in its own right as a NC subject. ICT covers various aspects or strands, such as control and handling and communicating information. Each of these strands is divided into levels 1–10. ICT NC is an entitlement for all pupils, although many schools are short of computers and have to struggle to meet the demands of ICT NC. Cross-referencing subject requirements with ICT capability, along with the practical issues of availability of hardware and software, means that the ICT coordinators have a mammoth task when formulating a planning document. As a result, schools face a stiff challenge to deliver ICT capability and often cannot spare computers for specific students, or for specific software systems. Schools are on a very limited budget and this needs to be borne in mind.

However, ICT NC capability is ideally designed for the dyslexic individual and, when learning ICT, dyslexic students can enhance their cognitive functioning in a manner which offsets their dyslexic tendencies. The skill is to know the cognitive strengths and weaknesses of the dyslexic students and marry that into ICT capability. So while ICT NC is being delivered, the needs of the dyslexic student are capable of being met. All of this results in greater independence, leading to greater self-esteem and self-confidence. For once there is an upward spiral instead of the usual downward vicious circle of branding and social withdrawal.

NC constitutes the majority of teaching time per week in schools. Very little time is left for extras such as celebrations, dental inspections, summer fairs and other activities. There is always a shortage of available time because teachers are under pressure to cover all aspects of NC within the normal school week. This never leaves enough time for the additional extras that happen. Therefore, the individual needs of a small group of pupils, such as dyslexic pupils, are best met within the NC framework. It is fortunate that this can be done.

The dyslexic student and access to NC in all subjects

Dyslexic pupils do not have equal access to the curriculum, for they are often unable to make notes and if they do so, they cannot re-read them. Consequently, what they tried to write is a waste of time. They are typically disorganised and cannot remember the lesson content if they rely on their memories. They cannot copy notes off a blackboard for they make too many errors; this includes writing down homework and dates. They get into trouble for not finishing homework, but have no notes to write from and no idea of when the homework has to be completed. Add to this their inability to manage study skills; find relevant information and make suitable notes; build up acquired information into an assignment, and the insurmountable problems become apparent. All of the above presumes that the student who is dyslexic has managed to process the lesson content. Most dyslexics have a phonological processing deficit and cannot process speech at a normal speed.

When attempting to write an assignment, dyslexic students require some facilitation to obtain information and then struggle to cope with the organisation of the assignment itself, often becoming confused and frustrated. This is compounded by poor handwriting and weak spelling. The whole process becomes frustrating and demoralising. ICT can change most of this by:

- giving access to the curriculum of the subject;
- giving help to the pupil with dyslexia, e.g. helping memory functioning etc.; and
- giving ICT capability in its own right.

Importantly, if ICT is used creatively it will not only give access, but also self-confidence and experience. Used well, the use of ICT results in pupils overcoming their difficulties, for example with weak short-term memory, organisational skills and spelling. All of these will be dealt with in subsequent chapters.

Chapter 2

Hardware and software

In order to enable access to the curriculum one needs the computer itself. This consists of two parts: the physical equipment known as the hardware and the programs called the software. This chapter provides a demystifying introduction to these.

Computers are relatively new to society, at least as far as the majority of the population is concerned. Even now, some 20–30 years after their introduction into general industry, few people understand the technical details of how these machines actually work and, as a result, the rest of us view them with a little trepidation. Having trained teachers and other adults while at Hummec, I regularly dealt with the computer phobic, who often made up about 80 per cent of the training participants. Not surprisingly, misconceptions linger around computers, together with a fear of damaging them as they are still relatively expensive.

In general the older the person, the longer it takes for them to learn about computers and mouse control. A typical 5-year-old child usually takes very little time to learn to control a mouse (see p. 15) and appears to have no fear of a computer. A novice adult can take weeks to control a mouse and often has fear of the machines when using them for the first time. This is understandable given that they have to pay the bill to repair it or, even worse, explain to the ICT coordinator in a school what has happened. The 5-year-old has the luxury of not having to worry about such things. However, it does mean that often adults, particularly teachers or ICT experts, place unnecessary hurdles in the way of dyslexic students trying to use a computer, because of their own misconceptions and fears. The pupils rarely have such difficulties.

Jargon is an integral part of ICT and I personally love to look at jargon words. When my first computer arrived I took six weeks to take it out of its numerous boxes, for it was so expensive, being much dearer in relative terms than most present-day machines. My sons and pupils helped me. The latter offered to stay in at breaks to work out the software and then inform me how to use it! I was always very grateful, as I was so nervous. This alone raised their confidence. I have continued to learn from my pupils and sons ever since. They never cease to amaze me and only rarely do I ever touch a manual – or *Manuel*, as one of my students called it.

To help those nervous about machines, I will openly admit that, although the ICT coordinator in the school was very kind and helpful, he still managed to get me very worried about the RGB lead. Apparently I placed the computer monitor too near the wall and was in danger of damaging the RGB lead! I knew this lead linked the monitor to the BBC computer, but only later did I find that the RGB lead had three wires in it, one red, one green and one blue. That was all the RGB stood for. These three leads gave white on the screen. If one of the wires in this magical RGB lead was broken the screen colour would change, or lines would go across it. I was scared over nothing more than an iron flex! I then found they were £4.99 each, so I bought several and carried one in my handbag for security!

Much later, while Head of Hummec, I entered a classroom, saw a pink screen and immediately said, 'Ah! The RGB lead is broken. You need another.'

The teacher was amazed.

Essentially there are two types of industry standard machines used in schools in England. These are either PCs (personal computers, typically running Microsoft Windows) or Apple Macintosh, often referred to as Apples or Macs.

Hardware (the physical bits and pieces)

It is important not to get too concerned about the hardware requirements. Most dyslexic students adapt perfectly well to any computer, so the requirements discussed below are ideal situations and not prerequisites. This is only a basic guide to equipment essentials and requires one to define a *system*. This consists of a computer, a keyboard, mouse and monitor.

The computer

This often looks like a square box and can lie on the desk (as in Figure 2.1) or stand upright, when it is called a tower. The computer itself consists of various internal components but the ones you need to know are as follows.

Figure 2.1
Computer systems

1. **The hard disk** This is the internal storage inside the computer. The bigger the hard disk the greater the memory, or storage facility, of the computer. Think of this rather like a warehouse, with large ones and small ones all used to store things. The hard disk is normally referred to as Drive C.
2. **There is usually a Drive A** This is where one places floppy disks. In the days of the BBC computers, and mainframe computers prior to the BBC-type computers, disks were actually very floppy and measured $5^1/2$ inches in diameter. The jargon has been retained even though disks these days are $3^1/4$ inches and are more rigid, being in a plastic holder. They slot into an opening – the

floppy disk drive which is usually called Drive A. Before computers had an internal hard disk, there were often two drives, Drive A and B. (Drive B is now rarely to be found but the internal drive is still called C. This can confuse people as they wonder why there is a Drive A and C, but no B. The reason is mainly that it became obsolete when the 5½ inch disk became redundant.) Programs, known as software, were originally inserted into the computer via floppy disk.

3. **The CD player/drive** This is often denoted Drive D and is the bigger slot on the machine. It is into this slot that CD-ROMs are placed. Enhanced versions of CDs known as DVDs (Digital Versatile Disks) are now produced. These include real video capability and will probably supersede CDs in the next few years. Compatible drives can use either CD-ROMs or DVDs, but older CD players cannot play DVDs, although they can be replaced. DVD drives can read CDs but not vice versa.

4. **Sound card** This is an internal circuit board which has the ability to improve the handling of sound, typically allowing external speakers and microphones to be used.

5. **Graphics card** This enhances the computer's graphics ability, which gives a clearer image on the screen.

6. **Modems** These can be external (a separate box connected by a cable to the computer) or internal (inside the computer). The modem gives the facility to be able to send electronic mail (email), access the Internet (web) and send/receive faxes.

The monitor

The monitor has numerous names and can be referred to as the screen, the VDU (Visual Display Unit) or LCD (Liquid Crystal Display) panel. Some monitors have a flicker on them. Some students are more sensitive than others, to screen movements and this can make seeing letters more difficult. I have worked on old BBC VDUs and they were considerably worse than more recent monitors such as VGA, SVGA or Trinitron screens. The latter is the best screen for a desktop machine and needs to be seriously considered for a dyslexic student going into design work or studying design-related courses at a university. However, although Trinitron screens are good, LCD screens are improving considerably and are now available in larger sizes with excellent clarity, although at a premium in terms of cost.

Clarity of screen appears to be more important than size so it is not necessary to get very large monitors. A good size of monitor is 17 inches for general use. Settings and resolutions can be changed to suit individual students, so by reducing resolution, or by increasing refresh rate, flicker is reduced. Trinitron screens and LCD screens are more expensive and are not necessary unless the pupil is particularly sensitive to flicker. LCD panels, at present, are also more fragile and are not, in my opinion, suitable for younger children. They might not last as long as conventional monitors. It is unusual to buy a machine without a graphics card these days, so the aim is to buy one with at least 2/4 mb of video memory on board. This will give an enhanced performance.

Keyboards

Keyboards are important, especially when considering small laptops. Most dyslexics typically have coordination difficulties and so a full-sized keyboard may be easier for them to use than the laptop's built-in keyboard. The larger size enables their fingers to hit the keys more accurately and allows for greater accuracy in typing. Most keyboards have little guide markers on the **J** and **F** keys, which give guidance as to the location of the middle row of keys. I have never found any pupils to have difficulty reading the letters on the keyboards and I have used many different coloured keyboards and key lettering. However, I introduced ICT to one company who were quite categoric that the keyboard on the new computers had to be a particular type with lettering to be of a specific shape for dyslexic students. In my opinion this is erroneous, but this serves to point out the perceived difficulties that people unfamiliar with ICT might deem as important. My advice is to let the dyslexic student try without any suggestion of there being a difficulty, and see how they manage.

A problem I have noted with keyboards has been with some ergonomically designed ones that have the keys placed according to each hand position. The difficulty is that they do not all divide the keyboard in the same place, so on one I have a **B** on the right side and on another the **B** is on the left. This can be a nuisance when the student has learned to use one special hand for the letter **B** and has to swap.

Mouse and other interfacing devices

These are small gadgets on a long 'tail' attached to the machine. The mouse is used for controlling the arrow on the screen – essential for pointing and clicking on different regions of the display.

Even if dyslexic students have a coordination problem, they can usually still control an ordinary keyboard and mouse perfectly well. I currently work with some 112 dyslexic pupils per week. I have had experience of working with many dyslexic pupils using various types of computers, keyboards and monitors. This experience also includes various types of mouse, from the conventional kind, to pressure pads and tracker balls, all of differing designs, shapes and sizes. The students I have worked with have had no difficulty with these different input devices. However, I have had many teachers who stated that their pupils would experience difficulties. Once more this demonstrates perceived difficulties, as compared to actual ones.

An additional note about hardware is that it is important to check the specifications of machines for different pieces of software requirements. For example if one wishes to use modern Voice Activated Software (VAS) then a higher specification will be needed. Whatever is suggested as the machine specification in the software, it will be an absolute minimum.

Most systems purchased for home use, now have sound cards, speakers and microphones as standard. If you wish to use a computer designed for office use, you may need to purchase these as extras. Most sound cards are Sound Blaster compatible. This is the de facto sound card standard. Sound cards will be needed for use with dyslexic students to provide a multimedia (with text, sound and pictures all together) environment. Check that the system you purchase has all of this and, obviously, a CD or DVD drive. Apple Macintosh computers automatically have sound installed, plus speakers and a microphone.

It is also important to choose either PC or Apple Macintosh machines to buy and work on. This is because they are the ones that dyslexic pupils will use in university, college or industry. Consequently it is advisable to use one or other type throughout. Some individuals recommend other proprietary machines but the standard is either PC or Apple. Research suggests that dyslexic pupils are more likely than most of the population to use ICT when they leave school and so it is important that they are equipped with the necessary skills that they will need in future life. This principle of consistency also pertains to software, where industry standard software should be used. This ensures that the pupils will already be familiar with it in future and know best how to use it to suit their needs. This gives them equal access.

A typical minimum specification for a computer would be:

- Pentium III, or Celeron, or equivalent
- between 128–252 MB RAM
- between 500–700 MHz processor
- 20 Gb hard drive
- graphics card with 2–4 MB of video memory on board
- between 32 and 64 bit AWE Sound Blaster compatible card (for VAS include Duplex quality sound card)
- between 16 and 36 speed CD drive for CD-ROMs or 64 speed CD/DVD drive or 4/20 CD-ROM writer
- speakers
- microphone
- keyboard
- 17 inch monitor (SVGA or 15 inch LCD)

Generally Microsoft expect the minimum to be P III 500 MHz computers with 64 mb RAM for their new software. Please note that though in the first edition of this book, P II 200 MHz machines were the minimum standard and we were anticipating the arrival of 1 GHz (i.e. 1000 MHz) machines, now, a mere two years later, the minimum is 500–700 MHz and 1.5 GHz machines are already in the high street shops.

Software

Software refers to the programs. Throughout this book the generic types of software that are useful are mentioned. However, not all examples of the available software can be covered and so, when choosing software, there are a few basic rules that I apply.

Hidden menus

I avoid software that has hidden menus, where one selects the options, for the dyslexic individual gets lost and confused trying to remember where they have to go in order to do what they had in mind. Some software can have three or more levels of hidden menus. Always make sure that everything, or virtually everything, is available from the current screen on the computer. This complies with 'recognition rather than recall'. Jakob Nielsen uses this phrase and in most usability engineering texts the requirement is that one should be able to look at a screen to work out what to do, rather than rely on memory. This is particularly important for dyslexic students of all ages.

Derogatory noises in software

Dyslexic students use ICT because it is an area where they generally have not previously failed. It is helpful, supportive, facilitating and motivating. The students enjoy working with computers and naturally work well in this environment. However, some teachers and parents tend to choose programs that appear to work on the weaker cognitive areas of the dyslexic students, principally spelling and reading. Very often this software has been written and designed with good intentions and based on traditional teaching methods. In essence, the student usually gets three chances to get the word, or the task, right and then a derogatory buzzer, or some such noise, sounds. This can be most upsetting to the dyslexic pupils and can deter them from working. If there is an option to turn that off, then I would suggest doing so. If not, I rarely use that type of software as it is prescriptive, rigid and confrontational. Most standard types of software are passive, particularly those found in industry. How would you feel if every time you got something wrong, you heard a derogatory noise being made in response?

A lack of response from the computer could in itself signal that an incorrect answer was given, with a correct response having a positive and pleasing sound. Why some software writers and designers still insist on having a reinforcement of the negative type to emphasise to the pupil that they are definitely wrong is puzzling to me. It is obvious when a mistake occurs, so why not leave it at that? Most dyslexic students are intelligent enough to realise their errors, without having to be reminded of them so pointedly. Also, having such a derogatory sound overheard by their peers can be intolerable for them. One can argue that earphones could be used, but even then the dyslexic pupils do not like the negative feedback. They already have low self-confidence and need to receive praise for what they manage. Rarely does such software give an auditory praise sound. I feel strongly about this and I am also voicing the feelings expressed by my pupils.

Keyboarding skills

Many adults, especially those not particularly familiar with ICT and dyslexic individuals, view accessing the keyboard as a hurdle to be overcome. I have worked with ICT and dyslexic individuals for at least 15 years, using many computers and on a daily basis. This must have covered many individuals. I have yet to find any of them have any difficulty with keyboarding skills. I give my pupils a guided tour of what the computer can do for them and this so motivates them that they wish immediately to start work.

The keyboarding instructions I give to my pupils are to sit well and comfortably, with the keyboard clearly in view. They are then advised to use two hands on the keys with their head placed roughly centrally above the keyboard, so that they can view all of the keys. If they have good supportive software, including sound, then they are fully facilitated and can write immediately. Their speed soon builds up. I can type reasonably quickly, with touch-typing, but most of my students are faster at keying-in than me. I never viewed keyboarding skills as a problem and it has never been one. The student shown in Figure 2.2 was so competent after two months on a keyboard, that he enjoyed typing an assignment being dictated by a Y11 pupil – a wonderful method of cooperative working.

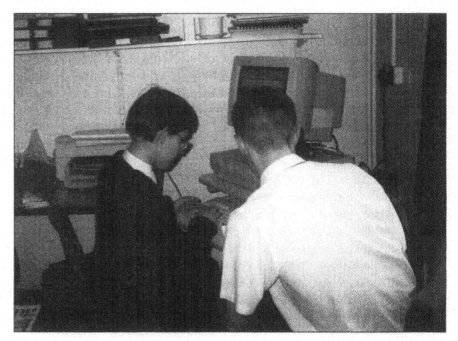

Figure 2.2 Keyboarding skills

I have asked a few students to trial specialist keyboarding skills software and give me their honest feedback as to whether it helped or not. Without exception they have discarded the software and preferred not to use it. They often found it as a barrier to the ICT facility and, on some occasions, it proved frustrating too. Very often if a mistake is made, the software decides which tasks have to be repeated.

If a parent or teacher insists that the pupil must learn to touch-type first, then there are manual systems that can be used on any appropriate keyboard, e.g. a typewriter. These systems allow greater empowerment for the pupils. There are typing course booklets, and these contain assignments and tasks for the pupils to work through. The pupils can use them while working at their own rate of progress. Instructions are given as to where to place the fingers, with appropriate diagrams. By using this method, I learned to touch-type perfectly well. I have also taught one university student using this method. She completed the course and could touch-type after only two weeks – though she was, admittedly, very keen to learn. Any old typewriter can be used for this type of learning or one can use a computer while still following the manual scheme. The advantages of this method are that the students remain in greater control and can better determine their own rate of progress.

ICT courses

Some teachers and parents immediately think that their child needs to learn about ICT on a specific course. This is not necessary if ICT NC is being covered correctly in the school. Most students will learn all they need within the normal school environment. Customising the software for dyslexic students is not covered on the majority of ICT courses, unless the tutor is familiar with dyslexic students and their particular needs. However, this need not detract from attending such a course, providing one does not expect it to cover the facilitation of the dyslexic student in particular.

Technology is changing all the time and when one looks at the progress made in computers, even from the BBC days to present machines, then one can wonder what the computers of the next five to ten years will be like. One needs to be wary of the latest developments. These are usually marketed well and some people just love to acquire the latest technology but they can be an expensive investment. For example, video conferencing systems were the latest technology only a short time ago but such systems are already, for the most part, obsolete because the same results can be achieved using the web. Software companies design the software for computers a couple of years behind the latest standards. One needs to be aware of this for it can mean that by upgrading your computer, the software you currently use might not work with the upgraded system.

Power and expense are not everything. The old BBC computers are still to be found providing support in many schools. At home we still use an Apple Macintosh LC, now at least nine years old, for administration. When looking for a computer one must first determine what is actually needed, the costs involved and the maintenance. In order to decide what is needed, one must look at the software to be used and the specifications listed. Buying a machine often constitutes a considerable investment both for homes and schools.

One needs to bear in mind that the hardware and software providers and retailers wish to make a profit. This means that obsolescence is built in to the retailing system. However, one need not always purchase the latest specification of machine, unless it is actually needed. Nor need one buy the latest version of the software. Good versions are available at a much cheaper price. One word of caution regarding software is that occasionally machines are sold with software installed. This can be a cut-down version of the software and it might not have all the functionality that one requires.

A final note for those students with acquired dyslexia due to trauma or accident: Don Johnston Special Needs Ltd specialises in software applications which have built-in scan and switch access features. There are also specially constructed mice and alternative keyboards which give access to people who are physically and/or visually challenged or impaired. These students are very important, although they constitute a small portion of the population. However, I recommend that students in this position contact Don Johnston at the address in the Appendix.

Summary

This chapter has looked at the most common components of a computer system in order to demystify them and show how each functions in relation to the whole. Dyslexic pupils often respond positively and quickly to using computer systems, fast realising the support, facilitation and access to a learning environment that ICT affords them.

Chapter 3

Where to start with ICT: portable solutions

ICT can be broader than simply using a computer. One popular misconception is that ICT only means computers and this is not true. The use of other technology, such as a remote control device for a television, is also included in ICT. One has to be practical and meet the needs of the dyslexic student in many varying environments within a school. Sometimes the low-tech answer is helpful and might be enough if the student has access to a computer at home.

Cassette recorders (Dictaphones)/ Digital recorders (minidisks)

The use of cassette recorders enables the teacher to record the important points of the lesson, freeing the pupil to concentrate on listening to the lesson. The recorders I use have two speeds so that they can be replayed at a much slower rate for dyslexic students. This means that the students hear each lesson's major points at least twice, once in class and again later. They can also retain this information for revision purposes, which gives them security and confidence. It reduces their stress levels. This system also ensures that if the dyslexic students have missed a lesson, they can still hear the content and not rely on second-hand written information that they cannot always process well.

The use of cassettes includes the teacher's intonation, which adds meaning. To support this system a teacher can produce handouts for the dyslexic pupils to use alongside the tapes, thus having two modalities for learning, listening and seeing. Spelling is assisted with this, along with greater access to the lesson content. Tapes are relatively cheap to purchase and I encourage the pupils to carry the tapes with them to each class/lesson.

Using cassette recorders is cheap and easy to manage, although I never give the recorder to the pupils. I insist the teachers or teachers' aides take control of the recorders. Very often tape-recorders are banned in schools, for obvious reasons. No teacher wishes every part of a lesson to be taped, nor do some pupils wish their private conversations to be taped. Consequently this method of technology needs to be sensibly managed. However, for parents, if this system is not in use in the school, it might help to suggest it. Parents can record notes to their children and the pupils can use cassettes to record important information they need.

Digital recorders, e.g. minidisks, are now available in many specialist audio shops and, to a more limited extent, in high street electrical retailers. They are generally more lightweight, smaller and fashionable, and parents may feel under pressure to purchase them. However, they are still noticeably more expensive than traditional cassette recorders and the disks/tapes are not as easy to play on other machines unless they are specifically supported.

Practical examples (from pupils at Foxhills School)

- One Y7 pupil disliked French lessons, as he could not process the words spoken by the teacher. That teacher recorded all of the phrases that she would cover during the lesson and included an English translation. This was also provided in written format. The pupil was able to access the phrases as often as he liked and felt much happier. The same phrases would be used for homework and he had a good and accurate record of the lesson content. From the tape recordings he could hear the words as often as he needed and was able to learn them as well as revise for a test. This still required a great deal of effort on his part, but meant that the learning process was possible.

- Another example was a Y11 pupil who was studying for English GCSE. He was Statemented for Specific Learning Difficulties, and struggled to write. He loved his English lessons due, in part, to a very talented English teacher. That teacher recorded the lesson about Shakespeare and the pupil used that recording as the basis for his assignment notes, which he typed up using Co-Writer, mentioned in Chapter 5 and Microsoft Word, mentioned in Chapter 6. This pupil also used the recording at a later date to revise the text prior to his GCSE examination. As a result, he was able to access the GCSE examination by being able to complete a 1,000-word assignment and revise for the examination itself. He repeated this process for other assignments.

Hand-held spell-checkers

Hand-held spell-checkers are small and relatively cheap for both parents and schools to purchase. I use those designed for desk or tabletop use because they are sloping and quite big, with large keys, for young children. There can be a few per class, say six, one for each group. A particular feature to consider regarding spell-checkers is how well the student can press the keys.

My older students like the spell-checkers that look like calculators or small credit cards, so that it gives them street cred with their peers. Peer equality rules the day for any teenager – just watch them all dress identically when it is a non-uniform day, each declaring they are stating their individuality (together). Such small machines have resultant small keys requiring the pupils to press the keys with a pencil or pen.

Franklin spell-checkers allow phonetic spelling, where the pupil writes the word as it is pronounced, although there are other spell-checkers that also cater for this type of spelling. If one types *fisicks* it should display *physics*. Some of the screens are not clear and the lettering can be displayed as tiny squares, giving an angular appearance. Some dyslexics find that hard to decipher and the interface should be examined before purchasing, so that a best match can be found. Equally, some come with dictionaries that are added to the price.

Most dyslexics hate dictionaries, often finding them confusing. As one dyslexic said to me, 'You have to be almost able to spell to use a dictionary and I can't almost spell!'

Some spell-checkers can have a foreign chip inserted and this allows foreign words and phrases to be used. It is usual to have one chip per language. Most of these machines have some word games, which can be very useful. In some models one can enter words of one's own choice, such as words for topic work, for science or some other specific subject, even examination PE! The pupils can then play games such as Hangman with these words. This is an interesting way of learning some words and, as it is portable, this feature can be accessed in any spare moment, such as while travelling in a car or during wet breaks.

Portable word-processors

Modern typewriters can be classified as portable word-processors. Typical models are the Star Writer, Canon, Brother, Sharp and Smith-Corona. These are typewriters with electronic features. The sentence being typed, or a portion of it, is displayed on a small screen. The document being worked on can be stored onto a disk and then transferred to a desktop computer. There are some of the usual editing features of a word-processor and these machines have a built-in printer. Their limited functionality is their biggest weakness. They do not take any other software and are quite heavy, so although deemed portable, they are not lightweight. They are relatively cheap and are often enough to meet the needs of the student for word-processing purposes. Many students, including those at university, use this type of machine and find it satisfies all their needs. The most recent models are improving all the time with added features.

Small dedicated portable computers

These may be laptops or notepads and are sometimes just referred to as word-processors. They are not to be confused with desktop PC replacements. Small dedicated laptops/notepads have been available for a number of years. Most are basically word-processors but they can have additional features. There are several different types dating back to the Tandy 100 series of about 10–12 years ago. Since then there have been many developments. The prices are relatively cheap and fall in a range for most families as a gift. Some of my pupils have organised various sponsored events to raise enough money to purchase these.

The laptops range in cost from £150 to £500, and they do not usually have a hard disk for internal storage of information. They have built-in software, can store a few files and are pretty sturdy machines. Some come with three-year warranties and the majority allow transfer of data to desktop PCs or Apple computers. Most of these machines have batteries or mains usage. This is important for invariably the only socket in a classroom is under the blackboard or in some other inaccessible place. Batteries solve this difficulty. The cheaper end of the market for these machines more than meets the needs of most students.

When choosing a laptop it is necessary to look for:

- a sturdy laptop that will take being rammed into a school bag;
- a lightweight laptop; these small laptop computers are usually quite light and this is an advantage; pupils often carry quite heavy school bags with lots of different equipment in them;
- clear screen display with adjustable brightness control;
- the ability to use foreign characters and mathematical symbols which students use in many subjects;
- a reasonable spell-checker facility. The spell-checker needs to be able to find the errors even if it fails to correct them. People often expect a great deal from a spell-checker. Do bear in mind that a spell-checker is dependent on the number of words it has stored as its dictionary. If these are few then it will not work very well. The more words in the dictionary the better. Therefore, it is wise to ask the number of words in the dictionary and thesaurus of any machine. If the spell-checker is not adequate I get my students to use the phonetic hand-held spell-checker alongside the laptop to get the advantages of both worlds (see previous section, p. 22).

Some laptops/notepads allow customisation of the dictionaries, allowing jargon and technical words to be added. Most of these machines have diaries and other organisational software built in which can be quite useful in helping dyslexic students organise themselves. All the laptops/notepads I have used allow printing to occur directly from them, so text does not have to be transferred to another machine. Indeed, I rarely transfer data for my students. This facility is more likely to be needed by supportive parents who wish to transfer a file to a home computer for storage.

If there is a danger that an older student might use up the available memory then I organise regular meetings when we discuss which files will be printed, which stored and which deleted.

These machines help students to:

- **re-read their own writing and notes;**
- **improve their organisational skills** – for instance their timetable can be entered on these machines, as can their diary along with their homework diary; the student can have other important information contained within the machine too, all of which helps them organise their time and study;
- **gain access to the curriculum** – students can use them to take notes in class; they can listen to the lesson content and note down what they need; my students use a mixture of cassettes, laptops and handouts from staff;
- **obtain printouts** – the text on the laptop can be printed straight

from the machine, usually on to any PC-compatible printer thus making a hard copy available; my students print out the first copy in large writing so that it is easier for them to decide how to edit; only when editing and amending are complete is the size of writing reduced and a final copy printed;
- **edit and amend ideas** – by spell-checking, using the thesaurus and cutting and pasting; this is done on the machine and another printout done.

This process results in reasonable and clear notes being available to take home for homework. Also homework tasks themselves can be printed off. Very soon, the students learn to touch-type and can then copy more easily from the blackboard as they do not need to move their heads from the one reading position. Greater access to the curriculum is provided in this way. These machines are useful for field trips and other outside activities for they are very mobile and portable. It should be noted that many of the general advantages of word-processing can be obtained via these laptops, including access to foreign language fonts and accents. Parents are usually appreciative of these machines, because they can actually read the homework assignments their children are given. Parents of dyslexic pupils are often totally unaware of what is happening in school and have no means of finding out without seeming to pester their children or the teachers. With readable notes and clear homework targets they are aided in assisting their children.

These little machines have provided a wonderful opportunity to some of my pupils and they love the freedom it gives them. The Head of English at Foxhill's School, wrote this note to me.

> Re: Dreamwriter:
> A boy called Daniel in Y11 has used Dreamwriter for just two months and in that time it has been a liberation for him. He is now able to work at his true level for the first time in his school career.

The following are some practical issues with laptops that need to be addressed:

- **Batteries and recharging** Some machines have rechargeable batteries and some have trickle-feed batteries. Some only work on ordinary batteries, but virtually all laptops work on mains electricity. Dyslexic students will need help in organising themselves to ensure the batteries are fully charged when they are needed and I keep a back-up of ordinary batteries for emergency purposes.
- **Security** These laptops are desirable and are portable. As such they constitute a security risk requiring sensible arrangements within a school.
- **Ownership** Are the students permitted to take the laptops home? I allow pupils over the age of 11 to use the laptops as they are required, which includes home usage. Younger pupils can find the responsibility daunting.
- **Maintenance issues** Some laptops have very good guarantees. Others are guaranteed for only 12 months and if they are broken after that length of time, then repair costs have to be met.

The above issues have to be resolved on an individual school basis, but are manageable. I have drawn up a contract that I get the students and parents to sign prior to their being given the machines. This emphasises that the laptops have to be treated carefully and lists the responsibilities of the pupil using the laptop.

These machines do not take additional software. They are cheap and cheerful, but suffice and deliver the goods. They are also easy to use and require little learning.

Portable computers

These are desktop computers with internal hard disk storage, in a small container. They have all the advantages of a proper desktop computer, for that is what they are. Unfortunately, these expensive computers are also called laptops, which can cause confusion. Some parents want these expensive machines for their children, but I would caution against this until the needs of the individual child are fully considered. If the child only needs to take notes and can then work later on a desktop computer, either at home or in school, they can manage perfectly well with a smaller and cheaper laptop/notepad, like those already mentioned.

A portable computer has the following practical problems.

- **It is more likely to break down** These machines are not generally as sturdy as desktop computers, although they are good. Dyslexic children are often clumsy too, and school life, with bags being thrown around, is not an ideal place for an expensive portable machine. What happens when the machine breaks down and the pupil is left without a computer? Has a spare to be provided?
- **It is expensive** With that automatically comes bigger security problems within a school. What happens if someone does steal it? What happens if someone accidentally breaks it, and this might be another pupil? Who pays, especially if it was a genuine accident?
- **Insurance usually has to be obtained** Who pays for this?
- **Ongoing servicing/maintenance** Who pays for this?
- **Additional software or upgrade software** Who pays for this?
- **It is heavier than a dedicated portable computer** The weight of the machine, plus carrying case, plugs, cables, leads and interfaces, can be considerable and some schools require their pupils to walk long distances. Together with the normal bag that pupils carry, it can be a significant weight.
- **The screen is generally smaller** This can be inadequate if the student is older and needs design type software. These laptops will need to dock on to a larger monitor, which has to be purchased.
- **Implications for teacher and parent training** If there are problems with the software or laptop in a classroom, not all teachers will be able to help and they might also feel threatened if they are not apparently able to cope. They might not be able to spare the time for the dyslexic pupil at that point in the lesson. Parents might not be able to assist their child. Some of the machines, and their sophisticated software, require a considerable learning curve for the pupil, the parent and all the teachers involved with teaching

that child, otherwise it is like giving a teenager a car and no driving lessons. Some will learn but others will have accidents that can be devastating, as well as expensive.

For older students at university they are a sensible possibility, but for younger ones they are not always the benefit they appear. The student at university might prefer a laptop because it can be locked away safely, it is mobile when travelling home for a holiday and can be taken into lectures. The downfall is that they are easily stolen, less sturdy, have a smaller screen and can be forgotten and left behind after lectures. Dyslexic students are quite forgetful. This does not rule them out for younger students, but the practical issues need seriously to be considered. The practical issues mentioned here are the result of my own personal experience with pupils.

Summary

Throwing money at a problem and buying the most expensive machine does not necessarily provide the best solution. Effectively, there is no substitute for a sensible, practical approach, offering appropriate support in a manageable and feasible way.

Chapter 4

Desktop machines and software

Desktop machines are limited in number and access to them in a school is for all students. Their usage is to provide access to NC for all pupils and so is generally prescribed. The planning within a school both for NC subjects and for the ICT component is structured, rigid and highly integrated into the medium- and short-term planning within every classroom.

One needs to balance the benefits of ICT with the reality that computers are not available for every child at all times. Therefore, access to the computers has to be rationed within a school and it has to be done fairly. Each child is entitled to NC, but none is entitled to more than the rest. This includes dyslexic students. Few schools can afford enough machines to deliver ICT NC capability completely and have computers to spare. Given the high demand, making available a computer for individual use is not always possible.

However, some pupils are Statemented for dyslexia and that Statement carries a monetary value. Particular schools use that to purchase computers and/or software. Many parents now provide computers at home and several schools operate a homework club. The schools I work in do. This means that pupils can reserve a computer for their own use after normal school hours. This chapter looks at the standard operating system on a desktop machine, how to use it and how to begin to tailor it to meet the needs of the dyslexic student. The second part of the chapter deals with where to begin when choosing software.

The standard operating system and some adaptations to suit individual needs

Modern computers have an operating system based on a graphical (GUI) interface. This means that it is based on pictures, referred to as icons. These require a limited need to read, with the exception of the Start button. This operating system comes with applets (tiny programs that are usually activated by one click of the mouse) that include the following.

- **Built-in calculator** This can be accessed at any time, via the Accessories folder in Windows or on an Apple via the Apple menu. Most computers have the toggle facility so that one can select an ordinary calculator or a scientific one.

- **Calendar** Also accessed via the Accessories folder. Typically it offers a day or month view and one can move forwards or backwards through the months as required. This facility also provides the current day and date.
- **Alarm clock** Students can use this to remind themselves of deadlines.
- **Diary option** This will help with organisational skills and time management which are essential for good study skills.
- **Clock facility** This can be turned on, thereby being visible on the screen and enabling dyslexic students to be aware of the time while they are working. The time is usually displayed in the box at the bottom right of a PC. By double-clicking on this box with the left mouse button, the clock will be fully displayed along with the calendar for the current month.

There are built-in accessibility functions to assist with the physical interaction with the computer. For example, if the student is clumsy and uncoordinated they might have difficulty managing to press two keys together, such as the shift key and a letter key to give a capital. If this is the case, one can have a sticky key function. This enables the child to press the shift key first and then the letter key. This option is available in Windows from the Control Panel where one selects the Accessibility options. In this area, click on the sticky key option. The Control Panel can be located by double-clicking on the My Computer icon.

Some dyslexic pupils will hold their fingers on a key for a long time and the computer misinterprets this as several key presses, often resulting in a long row of the same character. To stop this happening, go to the Control Panel and again select the Accessibility options. Choose the option to filter the keys.

If the pupil is left-handed, or wishes to use a left-handed mouse, then from the Control Panel click on the mouse option and change it to a left-handed one.

One can also change the tracking rate of the mouse and so on, to customise the settings to suit pupils with different needs.

There is the possibility of choosing a larger arrow for the mouse, and some computers have the option to choose different icons, such as a hand with a pointed finger.

All of this is easier on the home computer, or on a computer dedicated to the one individual. It becomes more difficult in a school environment, particularly on networked machines, which might not allow access to these features. However, the possibility is there.

Types of introductory software

Using good software for ICT is facilitating and it is a wonderful means of accessing the curriculum, which reduces stress both at home and at school. It enables the dyslexic to work at an appropriate intellectual level and experience success. It reduces frustration and lowers stress by empowering the student. However, computers and computer software will not solve dyslexia. Computers cannot teach. Just watch any true dyslexic who knows ICT and watch them cheat the system. Most know how to press a certain key until the computer tells them the answer, or they find some other way of solving the problem. I have given my son many pieces of software designed to teach spelling, or some other skill, and asked him to learn nothing but to complete the program, including the appropriate printouts. He has nearly always managed to do this. I now do the same with my pupils and they have yet to be beaten by any software. It is important to check that the child is learning while using ICT and not simply sitting watching words while not really learning at all. A child being entertained and appearing to enjoy him/herself does not mean they are actually learning.

When looking at software, do not automatically dismiss American software. I have never found any problem with the pupils using this as they are so accustomed to American TV programmes. Some teachers have complained to me about American accents, but what really constitutes an English accent? A great deal depends upon where you live. Most software now comes with English dictionaries and English customisation, although you might like to check this before purchasing.

It is important to buy software from only reputable companies, for there are dangers with viruses. Indeed, for a home computer, it is best to install a virus protection package. Most software packages come with a licence that allows you to download free updates to their anti-virus records from the www. This is important because a virus-checker that is out of date will not be able to combat new viruses, such as witnessed by the CODE RED virus in August 2001. Virus companies are generally very good at finding ways of stopping new viruses and often have 'cures' for them in days. However, you can only get the 'cure' on your computer if you actively fetch it. It is, therefore, good practice to update your virus-checker on a regular, fairly frequent basis.

For practice in using the mouse and to introduce the child to work with a computer, I usually start with software like one of the Living Books series: *Broderbund* (REM). The child is presented with a multisensory environment, listening to the words, watching them and then being able to interact with the page on the screen. The stories are amusing and the supporting materials with the software are very useful. The child is working at Level 1 of ICT NC but the Living Book also marries into NC English quite well, so its usage is more than justified. This Living Book software also comes with the book to sit and read to the child. Any means of helping to redress that imbalance in reading words created by dyslexia is useful. These Living Books have a Spanish option as standard, so are useful for older pupils learning Spanish as a Modern Foreign Language (MFL).

For older students and adults, there are games provided free on the standard operating system. These provide an entertaining environment in which to learn mouse control.

Games software

Playing games is not always a waste of time, although much depends on the type of game chosen. Some games are useful to assist with coordination skills requiring good hand–eye coordination. Parents and teachers can be quite selective, as there are many games available, so if one objects to a particular type of software, there are often more suitable alternatives available.

Some games, however, are useful for modelling and for simulations. This is one of the strands of ICT capability. Titanic Adventure Out of Time *Europress* (REM) is one such game, where the student learns while playing. There are many games of this type, which involve problem solving, hypothesising, logical thinking and other skills such as discussion work and cooperative working. Certain games therefore deliver ICT NC capability. A few educational software suppliers that provide games software, along with many other types of software, are REM, TAG and RM. All addresses and telephone numbers are included at the back of this book, along with further suggestions of appropriate software. Software is continually being developed and it is impossible to preview and use all of the available programs, and so please note, the ones mentioned in this book are as a guide. Throughout the chapters I offer direction to parents and teachers regarding what to look for when buying software.

Art packages

Most art software is a wonderful tool for dyslexic individuals and teachers. MS Paint is available from the Accessories option on PCs.

I use Kid Pix Studio *Broderbund* (REM) because it is a multimedia art environment, but other packages would suffice. It incorporates sound, art and text all in one environment, with extension facilities, too. This software is usually affordable for both parents and schools.

Kid Pix allows one to listen to the brush as one paints. Sound echoes the movement of the mouse and each brush has its own individual sound. The children can hear the square being drawn and the movement of their hand elicits an auditory feedback. This helps their coordination skills and they often become engrossed in what they are doing. The various aspects of Kid Pix include video *snapshots*, which can be added to the pictures along with text and recorded sound. There is a built-in recorder and one simply says the sentences one wishes to record.

To create a picture, the pupil draws electronically while listening to the sound. If they cannot draw what they wish, or lack confidence, there are many *stamps* available. These consist of small icons that are merely stamped onto the screen. The size and colour of the chosen stamp can be changed, along with their orientation. A footprint can be made to point in another direction (useful for Treasure maps). When the picture is complete, the student might wish to incorporate a moving image. This is easily done by choosing the one you want and inserting it.

Recording sound in this manner is advantageous for the dyslexic student. To think of a sentence, remember it, practise it and then record it is, in itself, a considerable task. It requires pupils to remember a reasonable amount, and this stretches and exercises their short-term memory. Accomplishing the task adds confidence.

Figure 4.1 is a story written by a 6-year-old who was learning the NC requirements for English, by writing a story with a beginning, middle and an end.

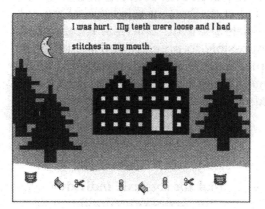

Figure 4.1 Oliver's motorbike story

After completing this he asked me, 'Which is the most important, the beginning or the end of a story?'

I asked him his opinion.

He sat and thought about this for a while – and sat still too, not a thing he did often. Then he almost shouted, 'The end!'

I was surprised and asked what he meant.

He said, 'The end is most important, because without it the story would go on to infinity and you would want a gigantic book!'

Curriculum uses for Kid Pix

- **Creating a single picture** – such as a treasure island map; a map in general of a route to school; a picture about a school trip.
- **Writing a story** – the stamps are of different sizes and so perspective can be added; a horse can be at a distance, by using a small sized stamp, and then get bigger as it is nearer, by using a larger sized stamp; different pictures represent different parts of the story.
- **Writing a poem** – poetry is an environment where one can express one's feelings; different verses can be written in different pictures, so that longer poems can be written if required. Many dyslexic pupils find learning a Modern Foreign Language (MFL) very difficult and one day Thomas arrived feeling unhappy. I asked him to express his feelings in the form of a poem. See Figure 4.2 for what he wrote.

- **Creating an advert** – this can be a multimedia advert, with text, sound and graphics.
- **Study skills** – such as timetables (see Figure 4.3) and flowcharts to assist with study skills (this idea thanks to Carol Kaufman, BDACC).
- **Illustrations for text written in a word-processor** – the pupils use the pictures created within their assignments to illustrate a topic; this type of work can be done at home, which is very useful.

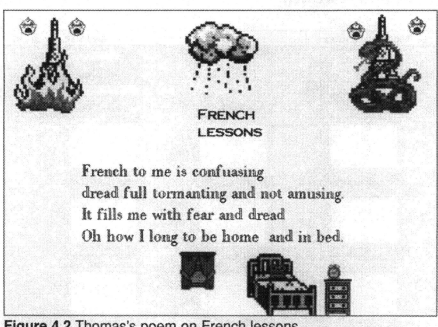

Figure 4.2 Thomas's poem on French lessons

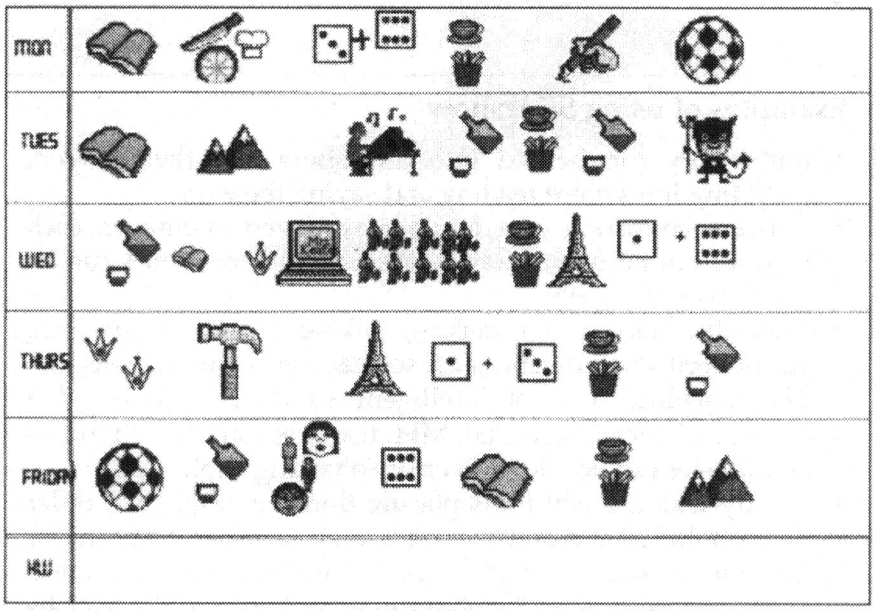

Figure 4.3 Timetable for Y9 dyslexic pupil

Extensions to Kid Pix

Within the Kid Pix software, there is an added facility called Slideshow.

As Figure 4.4 shows, this looks like a screen of lorries and you can load onto a lorry a picture that the child has previously created and saved. Sound is either added at this stage, or the original sound can be used. You then choose how this picture or screen will fade into the next screen. If you place the lorry in the wrong order, you can just pick it up and move it, thus editing and rearranging the work. This is a multimedia environment yet is easy to use. Dyslexic pupils can create moving adverts, cartoon stories, talking stories and other multimedia presentations. My students of all key stages use this software very effectively.

Figure 4.4 Slideshow screenshot

Examples of using Slideshow

- Jim's story can be fed into Slideshow and then played, including Jim's voice reading and saying the words.
- A poem consisting of a few verses, a verse being on each picture, can be placed into Slideshow and the verses can be played consecutively.
- I use this facility for making talking books of my own, customised for different ages, so that the context is relevant. The machines are not intelligent so do not know what language is being recorded. MFL teachers can record phrases and images can be added to create a talking book.
- The dyslexic student finds placing things in sequential order difficult. In order to assist, you can make a series of pictures or illustrations which could be factual, e.g. how to make toast. These can be placed in Slideshow, and their order can be

muddled up. The task for the student is to arrange them in the correct sequential order.

- One geography teacher made a slideshow to demonstrate the erosion of rocks from the coast and also to demonstrate the water cycle, all with suitable commentary.

Summary

This chapter was designed to stimulate ideas and to introduce software, including the software that my students and I find easy to use. However, I must emphasise that although I particularly like Kid Pix Studio, there are many other types of art packages on the market. Equally the extension ideas of moving images and multimedia environments can be achieved by other software such as Hyperstudio *Roger Wagner* (TAG).

Having made a start with this type of software we can now develop the ICT skills further.

Chapter 5

The writing process

This chapter looks at the use of word-processing to support the writing process.

A word-processor is a generic name for a program that allows the entry of text. As already explained, dyslexic pupils have difficulty writing, reading back what they have written, placing things in chronological order, editing and amending their work, thinking of the words they wish to use and how to spell them. All of these skills are supported with word-processing, in addition to the writing process as a whole. The methodology presented in this chapter is useful both at home and at school.

Essentially, a word-processor is not a means of printing. I have witnessed both parents and teachers who were not familiar with ICT getting the pupils to handwrite the article and then type it into a computer ready for printing. One must always question whether the use of the computer is justified. They are expensive machines and a typewriter would suffice as an alternative if one merely wished to have a pretty printout. The ICT skills are not being enhanced and NC is not really being delivered, apart from possibly saving the work and reloading it at a later date.

Essentially, word-processing is best done in its entirety from first planning through to final product. That is how it was designed to be used.

When asking a pupil to write a document, the child lists all of his/her ideas, then moves up and down the document (scrolling) to insert more text or to delete unwanted text. After the initial planning is done, I get the pupils to print out what they have written, with further regular printouts throughout the drafting and redrafting process. Modern word-processors have word-wrap, so that the student does not have to note the end of a line, but just continue typing and the words automatically go on another line.

At this stage, and throughout the creation process, the student is encouraged to work in a large, but clear, style of writing character, called a *font*. Most printed letter 'a's look like upside down, mirrored 'e's. This is confusing for some dyslexic pupils, so I suggest they choose a font style that has a good printed letter *a*. Sassoon Primary (REM) is a good clear font, and there are several others. The size of a font is measured in 'points' and I advise the pupils to write in a font size above 16 point, with younger children using sizes up to 20 point.

One can also colour the writing, and again this is quite useful. Working with the pupils we select which colour gives the clearest writing on the screen and the sharpest edges. Figure 5.1 shows a few examples of fonts and sizes:

Arial 18	Arial 12	CREEPY 22	Comic sans 18	Impact 18	ASHLEY 12

Benguiat Frisky 18	BERTRAM 18	Broadway 14	Eraser dust 18
ECLIPSE 18	Harlow 18	YEARBOOK OUTLINE 18	traffic 18

Figure 5.1 Examples of some fonts available

This demonstrates just a few of the many fonts that are available. Pupils can easily alter the presentation of their work simply by changing the font options or properties. They can make their work easier to read, thus making it easier to edit.

Once the text is planned and entered into the word-processor, it needs to be saved as a document file. Dyslexic students invariably forget what they called a document and so I find it advisable to assist them in devising a system that will help them and one they will remember. This is important both at home and at school. Do remember to save the document regularly. If it is an important document I advise regular printouts using different names for the different versions, e.g. doc v1, doc v2, etc.

The basic strategy is to get the ideas down on paper, by encouraging the creative flow with minimum distraction from this. *Then* edit and correct it.

We discuss what has been written, usually by printing it out first. At this stage we discuss the title, to ensure that the pupil is aiming correctly at what is actually required. Then we further discuss what is needed to effect the changes. After this discussion, the text can be altered and the document re-saved. This process can be repeated, if required, and further amending and changing can be done until the document is slowly built up. During these creative stages it is very important *not* to check the spelling and to let the pupil use words they would normally wish to use in ordinary speech, excluding colloquial terms. After working in this way a few times, the student soon learns the process and can do this unaided.

Some editing will have occurred while the text was being written, for dyslexic pupils often change their minds during the creative process. When the whole of the text is entered and the content is complete, we can amend, edit and redraft what has been written. I have found from experience that if a dyslexic student tries to concentrate on the content and also on how it is written, this can be confusing. It is more productive to concentrate on one task at a time.

The benefit of word-processing is that it enables one to do just that. Pupils may wish for another printout at this stage: editing on a screen is much harder for dyslexic students, as they do not spot the errors so well. The pupil is now free to concentrate on punctuation, grammar and other editing features.

Amending is easily achieved by any modern word-processor, as inserting and deleting text is a fast, easy process. To insert text the student moves the cursor, clicks the mouse button at the appropriate place, and then inserts the letters, words or sentences they wish. To delete text, they click again with the mouse at the appropriate place, and press the delete or backspace key.

Finally in the writing process, we look at the spelling and use the spell-checker. It is important not to place too much faith in the built-in spell-checkers of most word-processors, as they are not designed for dyslexic pupils. The spell-checker will not always be able to help and is not intelligent in the usual sense of the word. It therefore cannot know if one has a homonym, and is incapable of knowing if the word fits into the sentence. I remind my pupils that computers on general sale are not intelligent. Having said that, the spell-checker is very useful and has resulted in many of my students improving their ability to spell.

Jim wrote the following (Figure 5.2):

> Daws Pi cvbr,
>
> I gfyk to sdgh khgfss sfdh. I am 9 yedfg asdy and A haser bhgy a fghj oghf ghfrbhger tyuhg fghty cghyr stgfa I was 3.

Figure 5.2

He was delighted with this and thought it looked really splendid. However, I noted his 'unusual' spellings and asked him to dictate to me what he had written and what else he would like to add. This was the result (Figure 5.3):

> 29th January
>
> Dear Paul Criton,
>
> I go to ######## School. I am nine years old and I have been a fan of Grimsby town Football Club since I was three. I am your best supporter and I attend as many matches as my dad will pay for, no matter what the weather.
>
> When I am not at school, I play football all of the time. I got some Paul Criton gloves for Christmas and I have a football which is all mine. I love football and I think Grimsby Football Club are the best.
>
> I have got your autographs and this is my most treasured possession. I keep your programmes as well. My friends think I am mad supporting you, other than for David Palmer, who has more sense because he supports you as well. You are my best player and I want to be like you.
>
> Your best fan,

Figure 5.3

Jim is a typical dyslexic and as diplomatic as they often are. I soon realised that he had the first letter of every word correct and the rest was pretty much gobbledygook. I asked him why this was and he said, 'If there are nine letters in a word and you get them all wrong, then it is marked wrong. If you work really hard for two hours and get eight letters out of the nine correct, but one wrong, it is still marked wrong, so why bother? I don't.'

I did say to him that I had noticed. However, his logic was perfect. It also mirrored previous research I had done for the National Council for Educational Technology (NCET). During that research I worked with four children, all of whom were dyslexic, and all hated attempting to spell words. While using a word-processor they found that the spell-checker was more likely to find the word they wished to write if they got the first three letters correct.

This was a very powerful incentive to get those letters correct, and the nearer one is correct in the spelling, the more likelihood there is of the spell-checker coming up with the desired word. This helps the child to be motivated to learn some spellings, or at least make a better attempt at the word. It also provides context-led spelling, which the child actually needs, and not merely lists of words for spelling tests. Such lists are not necessarily going to be used and get forgotten rather quickly.

The result of the spell-checker help, resulted in the children being more willing to use words that previously they would not have attempted. At this stage the advantages of word-processing are worth noting. The pupils are able to use words and language that better mirror their own speech. I have found that dyslexic pupils often wish to write a word, feel they cannot spell it, and so choose an alternative word that they are able to spell. The result is that their writing does not represent a true picture of their vocabulary and their normal level of language usage. Instead their writing is restricted and can appear immature.

After the editing is complete, we go through the text together and note any repetition of word usage, such as *beautiful* being used more than a few times. The thesaurus is utilised at this stage and alternatives are sought; for example, *lovely, attractive, exquisite* are possible replacements for *beautiful*. The document swiftly becomes more enhanced and complete.

Part of my NCET research also provided me with a resourceful use of the thesaurus by one of my dyslexic pupils, David, and it is a method that I have passed on to many dyslexic students since. David wrote *bag* and then highlighted (a difficult term, for in fact highlighting is typically black or coloured) the word as if to check the spelling. I asked him why he was doing that as he had spelt it correctly.

He said that he wanted to use the thesaurus, did so, and this brought up alternative words for *bag* including *satchel*. He inserted *satchel* and said that was what he wanted to write but did not know how to spell it. The thesaurus helped him!

This typifies the lateral thinking and ICT usage that dyslexic pupils have. I have had to learn to think like them.

It is the thesaurus that helps with homonyms and synonyms. The pupils can check the word written with the thesaurus and it will give the meaning, by giving similar words to the one chosen. So if one writes *sea* the thesaurus comes up with *ocean, wave*. If they meant *see* – to look at something, the students realise that they have the wrong word and so they can change it.

Text on the screen can be moved around the document. One way of doing this is via cutting and pasting which are useful tools/ techniques for dyslexic students. The student selects the text to be moved, highlights it and then cuts the words by clicking on the icon in the toolbar that looks like a pair of scissors. When cut, the text can be transferred to another location in the document. This is achieved by clicking on the paste icon that looks like a clipboard. The text is then inserted into the new location. Whole sentences and paragraphs can quickly be moved in this way. I use this facility more for the older students.

Recently we have been using the facility of cutting and pasting in the process of writing letters of application. I first discussed with the pupils what type of information was requested in letters of application for jobs. From this we created a file consisting of a bank of sentences that might be useful, appropriate and tailored to typical qualities sought after in job advertisements.

From this bank of sentences the students could select the ones that they wished to use. I showed them how to highlight, copy and paste these across into a letter template, personalising it by using their own names, addresses and other information already entered. This process saves a great deal of time and provides a high-quality product.

By using the search and replace tools one can speed up the keying-in process for older students. I encourage my students to use abbreviations for long words, e.g. *ent.* for *entrepreneur*, initials for someone's full name, e.g. *Sh.* for *Shakespeare*. When the document is complete, they can use the search and replace facility to instruct the machine to search for each instance of *Sh.* and replace it with *Shakespeare*. There are a few things to be wary of, in that if one is not careful in selecting what to replace, then the machine can replace each *sh* in every word with *Shakespeare*. It makes interesting reading. However, I instruct the students to follow the word to be replaced, in this case *sh.*, with a full stop. One can also make the search case sensitive. This means one can ask the computer only to replace *Sh.* where the *s* is a capital and the *h* a lower case letter. This seems to avoid most problems.

The advantages of word-processing for the dyslexic pupil cannot be over-emphasised. It facilitates the writing process for all types of writing. Dyslexic students usually cannot manage to handwrite a document, edit it and then rewrite it. They lose where they are, lose the content flow and get almost overwhelmed with the spelling. The whole process is too difficult, exhausting and frustrating. If they really struggle to handwrite a document and edit their work, it is often untidy and contains many mistakes. It genuinely represents their best attempt.

Pupils have handed GCE and GCSE assignments to me containing many errors that would have meant a lower grade examination result. As a teacher one is not permitted to correct and mark the assignment to be submitted as the pupil's own unaided work, so I would ask them to check it themselves and make any alterations or rewrite it completely if time permitted. Often they were too exhausted with the whole task and would simply say that they had really had enough and could not face working on it any more. However, with a word-processor, they simply edit the text on the screen using the spell-checker or thesaurus and the job is far less daunting. Consequently they get better examinations results and this applies to every subject where written text is needed, which is practically all subjects.

Other advantages of word-processing will be covered later. However, essentially a word-processor must have:

- word-wrap;
- spell-checker;
- choice of font type;
- size of font options;
- formatting features, e.g. *italic*, **bold**, <u>underline</u> etc.;
- search and replace facilities;
- thesaurus;
- desktop publishing (DTP) features, e.g. boxes for titles;
- illustration facilities;
- foreign accents;
- cutting and pasting; and
- sound facilities.

Most word-processors have many more features, but the above are essential for dyslexic students.

When the dyslexic pupil is entering text, *talking* word-processors give an auditory feedback. There are many examples of this type of software available and the one I use is WriteOutloud by Don Johnston. The features I particularly like are the following.

Talking word-processors

Background colour

I can colour the screen that the pupil is using to any suitable shade. On a PC version the colours are plain red, green etc. but on an Apple one has the choice of a huge range of colours. The options are incredible. If the child has Scotopic Sensitivity Syndrome and consequently wears coloured lenses in order to see the text more clearly, I can choose an appropriate colour of the screen that is the best match for that pupil.

Text colour

Text colour is available on the PC version as a straight choice of colour; however, once again on the Apple it has the same virtually infinite options available, as for background colour.

When selecting from the options of background colour and text colour, I encourage the pupil to tell me which colour combination gives the clearest text and the sharpest lines. This can make a considerable difference to some pupils. For those less affected, there is usually a preferred choice, and some benefit in clarity.

Voice options

As the pupil writes, the software will either say: the letters one by one; the whole word; the sentence; or the complete paragraph. One can choose whichever option is required. The voice options on the PC are good, although they do depend upon the quality of the sound card and speakers. On the Apple, they are superb. One can choose from many different voices; male, female, robotic, unusual and downright weird.

An example of using talking word-processors

I have used different voice options to advantage in that I have had two children on two separate computers. On one computer a robotic voice was selected and on the other a deep male voice was chosen. The pupils took it in turns to write the sentences and listen to the machine as it spoke the sentence written, in the selected voice. The robotic voice was an alien lost in London and the deep male voice was a London policeman. The dialogue had to be conducted via the computers and the children loved this.

This is an excellent method for creating role-plays and you can work with the children to produce a suitable scenario. The voice option can be speeded up or slowed down according to the phonological processing skills of the children. This is done via a number option on a PC but on an Apple one can choose 50 words per minute (WPM) to 500 WPM. Research suggests that robotic voices are better for assimilating than digitised speech (recordings of normal speech).

One 6-year-old told me that he had received a *bowanaragun* for Christmas. He meant a *bow and arrow gun*. He did not know that it was four words and had attempted to write it as one word. When I told him it was four words, his look was a mixture of surprise and disbelief. I had to prove the point by referring to pictures of bows and arrows. Dyslexic pupils often experience this type of difficulty and robotic speech helps them to separate words and particularly to hear the endings of them. This improves their phonological awareness and, subsequently, their spelling.

Dialects and local pronunciations are well catered for, as one can adjust the individual words. Some adults complain that software has an American accent, and it should have a British one. However, this software can be customised to match local pronunciations. Another advantage in using WriteOutloud is in assisting young pupils to use full stops. WriteOutloud will only read out the sentence if there is a full stop. Younger pupils soon learn this.

A talking spell-checker

The talking spell-checker will read the sentence that contains a mis-spelt word and then sound out the individual word, letter by letter. There are no hidden menus, and pupils find this software particularly easy to use.

The newest version of WriteOutloud has the Franklin dictionary, identical to the ones in the hand-held Franklin spell-checkers. This means that the dictionary is a phonetic one. The pupil can write the word as he/she would say it and the spell-checker is much more likely than non-Franklin spell-checkers, to manage to locate the correct word. This means that the spell-checker is very useful. By writing the word as they would say it, it helps the dyslexic pupils to listen to their own speech and to the sounds that constitute the word. This is helpful and they have a strong motivation for using the spell-checker because it will then support them. While doing this the pupils are using the words they need, context-led words, and as a result are more likely to learn the correct spelling because they will be needing the words again. By having auditory feedback the pupil is receiving confirmation of the spelling of the words.

Co-Writer (Don Johnston)

Co-Writer is a complementary facility I use alongside WriteOutloud (see Figure 5.4); however, it can be added to *any* industry standard word-processing software including Word, Word Perfect, etc. I use Co-Writer if students:

- are new to using a computer and do not have any keyboarding skills;
- have significant coordination problems; or
- cannot write independently because their spelling is very poor.

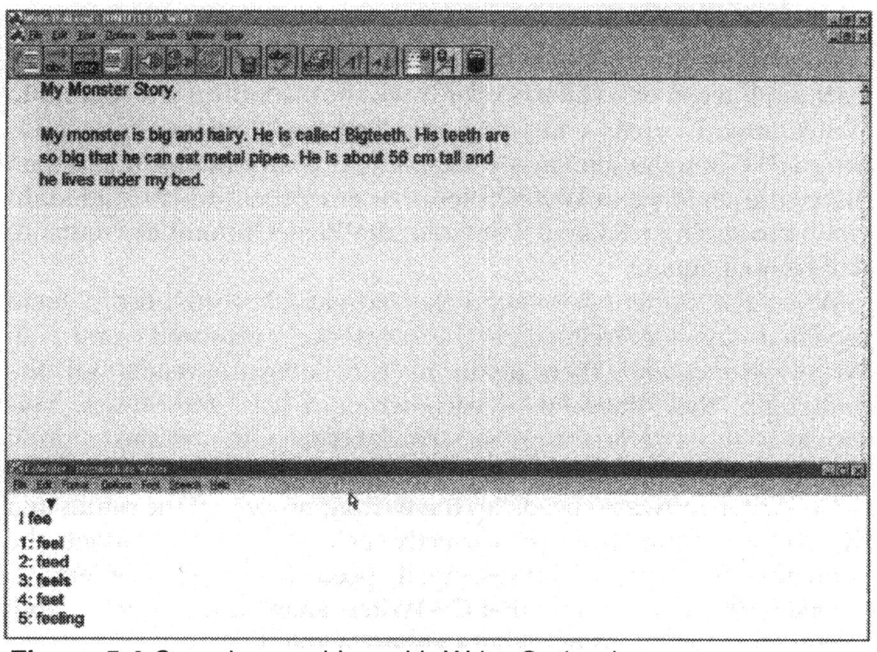

Figure 5.4 Co-writer working with Write Outloud

Co-Writer works by predicting what pupils wish to write from its bank of words. Co-Writer also has a built-in grammar facility. Pupils key-in the first letter of the word they wish to write. Co-Writer then selects from its bank of words the most commonly used words beginning with that letter. These are displayed on the screen. If the word that the pupil wants is listed, the pupil selects it either by typing the number alongside the word, or by clicking on it with the mouse.

If, however, the word is not displayed, the pupil keys-in the second letter of the word. This is usually enough for Co-Writer to suggest the correct word needed and the pupil merely clicks the mouse button or selects the number of the word, and it is chosen.

When similar-looking words are displayed to a dyslexic pupil, as is the case with most predictive software, the pupil might become confused and be unable to read the words. I have found this happens often. However, Co-Writer actually reads the words aloud to the pupils. This is done by pointing the mouse cursor to the list of words and, as the pointer is moved, the word is read aloud. When the pupil decides upon the word, Co-Writer enters it on to its screen and says it again.

Co-Writer offers the words likely to be needed and learns the vocabulary the pupil is using regularly. It works by giving words a prediction rating and the more often a word is used the higher the rating, i.e. it responds to frequency of use. A parent or teacher can give any specific word a higher rating if one thinks it is more likely to be needed, e.g. in advance of topic work with specialist vocabulary. New words can be entered into the dictionary, so specific subject words can be added. The grammar facility means that Co-Writer will also suggest appropriate words such as conjunctives and prepositions. This helps the student with sentence structure. Co-Writer now has customised dictionaries which are based on NC subjects and topics.

The ability to customise the software is considerable and it is impossible to cover all that can be done. Co-Writer also consolidates learning the use of a full stop, for it will not enter the sentences into WriteOutloud, or any word-processing package, unless a full stop is inserted. When the sentence is complete, Co-Writer reads it and then places the sentence in WriteOutloud, or any other industry standard word-processing package. If entered into WriteOutloud the sentence will be read again.

When the student has heard the individual words, heard them repeated by Co-Writer in the sentence, repeated again in WriteOutloud and then again as the software reads out the paragraph, they have heard each word at least four times. This provides the overlearning and consolidation the dyslexic pupil needs. As a result spelling and writing skills quickly improve.

Co-Writer software speeds up the writing process of the pupils and they know that the words are correctly spelt. For the new student who is unfamiliar with word-processing, it speeds up the entry of text.

One pupil's verdict was that Co-Writer 'enabled me to write what I actually wanted and not what I almost wanted'.

Pupils are encouraged to attempt words that they wish to write because they soon learn that Co-Writer will assist them in spelling the word. The quality of writing in terms of vocabulary and spelling increases considerably.

Very importantly, Co-Writer logs new words into a file and adds these words to WriteOutloud. One has the option to include these new words into the user dictionary, useful for technical terms. This option is extremely useful for it allows the adults working with the pupils, as well as the pupils themselves, to see the file of previously misspelt words. This demonstrates the type of errors they typically make and how their spelling is improving. This is also useful for diagnostic purposes, so that an adult can see what needs to be taught to the pupil in order to help their spelling. This file can be printed off too.

I have used these pieces of software with pupils from 4 to 16 years. After only six months the pupil mentioned above, Jim, was able to produce an unaided piece of work (Figure 5.5), by using these two pieces of software.

Monday June 24,
I played football with the Pilgrims in Immingham.
I won one game and I played good. It was good
because nobody was mardy. If I get picked I will
be in the team.
Clive Madonca is the footballer I want to play like
because he is the best player and he got a hat trick
against Ipswich. He plays for Grimsby Town.
I like to play cricket as well. None of my friends play
because they are gormless. Mydad played for Great
Coates cricket team but I have never seen him play.
He had an enormous bruise though when the ball
missed his padding.

Figure 5.5

Both WriteOutloud and Co-Writer are easily extended to cover physical access features for those with acquired dyslexia due to trauma or accident. The new AlphaSmart laptop has Co-Writer installed, which gives greater functionality to this relatively cheap, but robust laptop.

Once the text is entered into WriteOutloud it can either be printed as a finished piece of work, or it can be transferred into Word or any other quality word-processor, if required, so that the document can be continued on another computer.

Once again I stress that although this is the software I use with my students, the methodology can be used with other talking word-processors and similar supportive software.

Summary

The writing process is an area with which most dyslexics have a problem and supporting it should be a principal aim. This chapter has introduced software packages to assist dyslexic pupils with ICT and also provided a basic guide to the properties required of a word-processing package.

Chapter 6

Industry standard software 1: word-processing

Having introduced the concept of word-processing, the most commonly available forms are the industry packages, for example Microsoft Word (MSWord, or Word). People giving ICT support to dyslexic pupils often overlook these types of word-processors. This is in part due to the marketing of these products, which does not overtly suggest their suitability for use with dyslexic pupils. However, this does not mean that they are not of use, for they are extremely powerful and highly adaptable. They are also very flexible and are useful for pupils from KS1 through to university level and beyond. Word is the word-processing package that I am most familiar with, but most other industry standard software will include similar features.

Customising Word

Word has many options and facilities, and these are displayed in the menu bars and toolbars (see Figure 6.1). By clicking on these you make your selection.

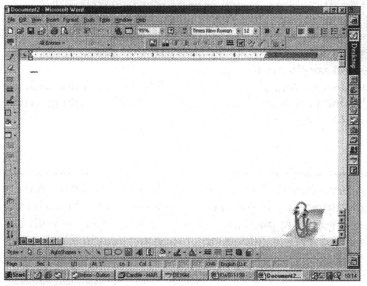

Figure 6.1 Screenshot of Word

Dyslexic pupils can choose their font type, size of writing, colour of text and so on, all by clicking on the appropriate icon on the toolbar or from the menu bar at the top of the screen. The text in Word can be coloured, as can the background screen. This allows for any visual colour preferences that dyslexic pupils may have.

I use the same method of writing, using a large font and a plain style, irrespective of the word-processing software in use. When children realise the many options available with fonts and the shaping of words, they often choose to write in a very complicated font, which they subsequently find incredibly difficult to read. This is unproductive, since editing their writing becomes difficult. I strongly recommend that a large, clear font be chosen for the creation process, with all the choices for style and size of writing being selected when the document has all of the text inserted.

Once the writing is complete, the children choose a font that best reflects the theme of their writing. If it is a scary piece of work, they could select a SCARY WRITING FONT.

If they have written about the Vikings, then a suitable font can be selected according to the pupil's choice. They often like an archaic style such as Olde English.

The following examples show how work was developed by a small group of 9-year-olds from a local junior school.

The first draft was then amended (see Figure 6.2) and, although it still contains mistakes, it was finally produced as shown in Figure 6.3.

First draft:

Sea rough windy breexy wet stormy

Second draft:

The sea was rough and it was a stormy wet night. there was a strong windy breeze that blew across the sea.
We wethe boat was slipery because it was wet. the boat had 12 oars and 13 sheilds,the figure head wa fearsome and scary.
We are the unwelcomeing scaryvikings. we are the edirty invaders. we kill and the villagers shout as we cut off their heads.   Theeere was a battle with swords clashing. Smelly blood filled the air. Glittering jewals and sparkling gold mixed with silver were found in a treaser shest.it was very heavy we struggle d to drag it to the boat.most of the way was uphill.
The village was abusy noisy place. with emlly dirty houses. we set the village ablze. it burened down.

Figure 6.2 Examples of the developing writing process

From this stage the document can be illustrated, a feature I will deal with later in this chapter.

It is impossible to express just how much a child can be impressed by a high-quality printout of a piece of work. One boy from a local junior school used the computer to produce a piece of work and printed it out. He looked at the printout and sat down with the paper

The sea was rough and it was a stormy wet night. There was a strong windy breeze that blew across the sea. The baot was slippery because it was wet. The baot had 12 oars and 13 shielda. The figure head was fearsome and scary. We are the unwelcoming scary Vikings. We are the dirty invaders. We kill and the villagers shut as we cut off there heads. There was a battle with swords clashing. Smelly blood filled the air. Glittering jewels and sparking gold mixed with silver were found in a treasure chest. It was very heavy and we struggled to drag it to the board. Most of the way was uphill. The village was a busy noisy place with smelly dirty houses. We set he village ablaze and it burned down.

Brenden the village slave had a stupid idea that he was the strongest man in the village.
The other men got angry and decided to challenge him. Firs they told him to toll boulders down a slope. Brenden did not succeed this challenge and the villagers jeered at him. The second challenge was to pull the Longboart out of the sea. The Longbaot did not budge. Brenden fell flat in the mud. After that he gave up. In the silent wood s next to the village two men were arguing valiently rolling ove the ground. Midnight was approachng and a wild board came out of the bushes and crept up silently. In a trice the men were gone.

We will report back when we know more.

Figure 6.3 Third draft which also demonstrates the use of fonts

still in his hand. He approached me later and asked for another printout. I showed him how to print a few copies. He said nothing more and went for lunch.

Later he arrived back at the classroom door and said, 'It looks real good, dun't it Miss?'

Even older students find large fonts useful. When completing assignments for GCSE, they often cannot manage to edit a paragraph well because they find a small font difficult to read. To overcome this, they locate the paragraph needed, highlight it, enlarge the font, do the editing and then select the original smaller font again.

An advantage of the text being a document on a computer is that one can do several printouts, so the pupil can take the work home, have a copy in school and a copy for display. Pupils can copy text from one part of their writing to another, by selecting it, choosing the Copy option, clicking where they wish it to be copied to, and pasting the text in. They can move entire paragraphs by highlighting the text; holding the mouse button down; scrolling to the desired position; and then releasing the mouse button. The text is moved by the word-processor. This enables the amending of text and placing it in correct sequential order, a facility regularly used by dyslexic pupils.

There are 13 toolbars to choose from in Word and one can customise each toolbar so that it includes the features one uses regularly. This allows dyslexic students to have the options they need easily accessible. Word also caters for most modern foreign languages. In addition, headers and footers can be added, along with page numbering. All of these features can be customised as required.

Word has an art facility so that illustrations can be included and one can also place borders around sections of text, to emphasise their importance. When the writing is nearing completion, pupils can look at a preview of how it will print out. As they write, they can choose to view the document in page layout. This facility enables the writer to see how the words are placed on the page and can move text around to suit individual requirements. However, this does often make the displayed writing very small.

As the pupils write, their documents are mapped so headings and sub-headings are noted by Word. It automatically corrects some words as they are typed, and it has a built-in grammar checker.

It is very important to note that I turn both the spell and grammar checkers off until the document is complete. Otherwise, it deters the dyslexic student who tries to spell a word only to have it immediately underlined in red, or green for the grammar checker. Some of my students have been quite upset at this, and yet will accept a correction when the work is done. In addition, I do not wish their writing process to be interrupted. It is essential that they can concentrate initially on content and then on spelling. This does not detract from the importance of spelling. Historically it was not always deemed to be so important and Shakespeare himself had no standardised spelling. Indeed, an English teacher of mine informed me that 'the dictionary was first collated for those of feeble brain who needed to spell the words the same each time'. However, spelling is regarded as important now and so good practice needs to be encouraged.

By checking the spelling towards the end of a document there are many advantages:

1. It allows the dyslexic pupil to write the content freely;
2. it allows the pupil and the teacher to note any regularly misspelt words;
3. it can be used diagnostically, so that I note similar spelling mistakes, such as not dropping the letter *e* when adding a suffix beginning with a vowel. This can then be taught and is context-led, so relevant;
4. in my opinion, it stresses the importance of spelling;
5. after the spell-checker, one can bring in the use of the thesaurus to improve the words chosen, and this will not work unless the word is spelt correctly.

Older students writing a thesis, or report, will need some of the more advanced features, such as linking to a spreadsheet, and the presentation features, such as text alignment and spacing. Word will count the number of words used and will also provide the use of customised dictionaries. This is useful for older students who need to have dictionaries of subject-specific words. Suffice it to say that Word has managed to facilitate all of my needs and those of my students, including those who have gone on to university.

Word also has sort facilities, where words can be placed in alphabetical order in lists, or in numerical order. How many teachers have written examination results and had to place the children in descending order according to their marks? After doing this, we often discover another child whose late inclusion results in most of the class being incorrectly numbered. In Word there is no problem, for it will just re-sort, and it does not make mistakes.

Few people realise that Word, if fully installed, can have sound inserted into it. Go to Insert on the menu bar and scroll down to Object. A dialogue box will open and from that select Wave Sound. A small cassette recorder dialogue box is then displayed. Press the record button and speak into the microphone. Cheap microphones cost about £5 and are adequate. Often the smaller and cheaper microphones are better suited to small hands, rather than the larger ones that look like large lollipops. When the sentence is recorded, an icon resembling a megaphone appears on the screen. This facility enables the teacher, or parent, to record sentences into the machine, one at a time.

If the students wish, they can record their own sound to help them.

Examples of using speech sounds in Word

- I have used this with students from junior school through to KS4. They simply record their sentences and then, by double-clicking on the sound icon, they re-listen to what they recorded (see Figure 6.4). This can be repeated as often as they wish. They slowly build up the sentence in written words without being hindered by having to remember the content, which is already contained within Word. This leaves them free to concentrate on the rest of the writing process.

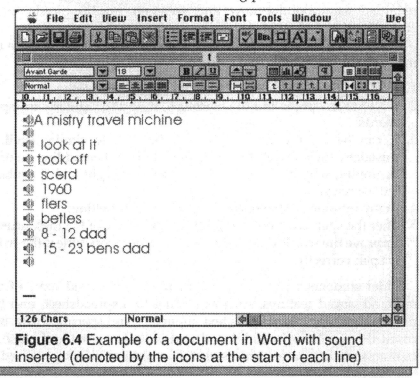

Figure 6.4 Example of a document in Word with sound inserted (denoted by the icons at the start of each line)

- Word will take recorded speech in any language. This enables MFL teachers to record phrases and sentences that the dyslexic pupil needs to hear often. This can be with text already inserted, or left as recorded sentences that the pupil can subsequently add the text alongside.
- Following a science lesson, the pupils can record what happened. It does not matter in what order the recorded sentences are done, so the student can record the end of the science lesson first, when they blew up the lab, then they can add the wonderful sordid details, one at a time in each sentence. Once recorded, it is easy to rearrange these sentences in a chronological order, by simply clicking on the icon and moving it. Sometimes my pupils need a word alongside the sound icon, so that they can use that to remind them which sentence is which.
- The voice facility is a fantastic help to most dyslexic students. If the phone rings, or the bell goes, and they need to add a final sentence in the text and time does not permit this, they can simply record what they wish to remember and it is there until they return.
- I get my students to record words that they cannot spell and then I can make a note of these spelling difficulties for subsequent teaching. One can also note the words recorded. Very often they are mispronounced, possibly resulting in the misspelling of the word. Often dyslexic pupils will confuse *th*, *f* and *v*. They can constantly mispronounce common words, such as *somethink* for *something*. These can be missed when the pupil is speaking but become more noticeable when recorded. Once noted, they can be dealt with.

Once the pupils have the text in files, they often wish to improve it by adding illustrations. At this stage they will have done the formatting and decided how they wish their work to look. For many dyslexic pupils this is a revelation in itself, for they have previously been unable to produce an attractive product and now they know how to. They are in a new and wonderful environment of actually deciding how their work will be presented and how to decide on its final format. They thoroughly enjoy this for they can gain peer equality, possibly for the first time. The sense of achievement at this stage is immense.

Illustrating the written text and further customising Word

Ways of illustrating text

These include the use of the following.

- **Pictures from an art package, e.g. Kid Pix or MS Paint** To do this, the pupils will have created their picture files in an art package and saved them. When using an art package one can highlight either the picture, or a part of it, and make a copy of it. Choosing the copy option within the software can do this. Open the target document in Word, and paste the art graphic into the document by selecting the Paste option in the toolbar. When pasted the graphic can be resized or moved to any desired position. Multiple copies of the graphic can be pasted in this way and added to each page. An alternative way of inserting graphics from an art package is to use the Insert option from the menu bar. One then chooses the Picture option and then select From File. It is necessary to know where your graphic file is stored. So before using this option, I get the students to save the pictures they wish to use on to a floppy disk. This ensures that they know where their graphics are and can locate them more easily. This also provides good study skills, for they have to arrange their work sensibly for easy access.

- **Graphics from the hard disk** Word comes with some preprepared graphics available for use. To obtain these, one needs to go to the Insert option in the menu bar. Scroll down to the Picture option and then select Clip Art. The software will automatically load a selection of pictures, providing Word was fully installed. From this selection, simply choose what you wish to use. Once inserted into the document, it can also be resized, moved around or copied many times.

- **Graphics from CD-ROM** You can purchase CD-ROMs with many graphics on them, usually several thousand images. These are relatively cheap to buy and are easy to use. You simply load the CD into the drive and then make your selection. These CDs come with a booklet containing all of the pictures. I find it easier and faster for my students to go through the booklet and make their selections first. This involves putting bits of paper in the correct pages and numbering them in the order they are to be used – again this encourages good organisational skills. Once this has been decided, the graphics can be inserted into the document and moved around appropriately. These CD-ROM graphics provide an infinite variety of illustrations including borders, lettering, backgrounds, cartoon characters and so on.

- **Scanned images** Scanners are relatively cheap to obtain and can either be black and white or coloured. They are also either hand-held or flatbed. The picture being copied is placed under the scanner and the scanner translates this into a file, which can be saved and subsequently downloaded into an art package or another piece of software.

- **Photographs** You can take ordinary 35 mm film photographs on any suitable camera. This film should then be taken to a good developer and a PhotoCD asked for. The photographs are developed in the usual way, so you get 36 photographs and also a CD. This has the photographs stored on it and these can be loaded on to your computer, whether Apple or PC. In order to edit the photographs, you need either special photo manipulating software – there are many versions available – or you can load it into an art package such as Kid Pix. The editing facilities enable one to take a small part of a picture, enlarge it, change it and so on. Existing photographs can be placed onto a CD-ROM. So one can take photographs of long-gone relatives and have these pictures digitised onto a CD-ROM. Resource CDs can then be made to support topic work in schools.

- **Cameras** There are special black and white or coloured digital-capture cameras. These work by automatically saving the pictures in such a way that the computer can immediately load them. This allows photographs by the students to be taken and used within the software.
- **From the Internet** Graphics can be loaded from the Internet to enhance topic work, or assignments. Students search for the graphic they want to use and then download and save it for future use. When inserted into Word, the graphics can be edited by resizing or moving around. Graphics downloaded into an art package can be edited more comprehensively, e.g. adjusting the colour.

The uses of graphics in software are many and varied. Essentially the prime usage is to enhance, and not just aesthetically, a document that the pupil has already written. After all, a picture can 'tell a thousand words'. Figures 6.5 and 6.6 are examples of this.

Many teaching staff can use word-processing facilities with graphics to enhance and develop worksheets. However, this is still a situation where dyslexic pupils potentially cannot read some of the worksheets with which they are presented if the sheets are of inadequate quality. This could be due to: the worksheet having writing that is too small; the sheet being handwritten; the sheet having been photocopied many times, resulting in loss of quality; or, for reasons of economy, an A4 original being reduced to A5 size, thus rendering it almost unreadable. In some schools I have been asked to help students with their homework and I could not read the worksheets. If the worksheet was saved on a word-processor, a good copy could be printed off as required and further copies made from that good copy.

For dyslexic students, individual words to learn can be typed into a word-processor in a large font and then colour-coded. These can be printed, laminated and made into **flash cards**. Flash cards are useful for teaching the reading of words. Parents can also make these types of cards for keywords for subjects.

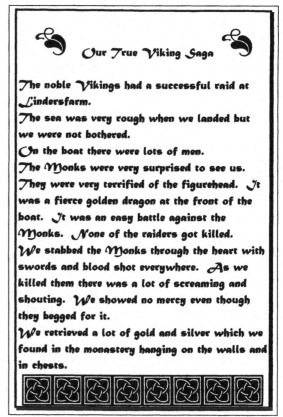

Figure 6.5 A document demonstrating the use of font and graphics for presentation purposes

Figure 6.6 An example of a graphic inserted to illustrate a poem. This pupil was aged 10

Specialised worksheets can be made for teaching individual phonics and work can be differentiated using a word-processor.

When using an Apple one can create **stationery pads** and **templates** on the PC. These are customised pieces of writing paper. Graphics can be inserted to form, say, a letterhead, or can go anywhere else in the document if required. The templates can be customised, for example, as a letter, a CV or a science experiment write-up. They can have coloured screens, coloured text and a font of a particular choice, with sound incorporated to be used as an aide-memoire. This customisation saves a great deal of time for the student as well as facilitating him/her, by reducing the lead-in time to producing the writing. Parents can also provide this customisation which will help with homework.

Word will work with more than one file open at a given time and it is possible to copy text from one file to another. Therefore, I have made sentence word banks for my pupils for different subjects, or topics, and had the file open along the bottom of the screen. The sentences can be colour-coded as required. They can also incorporate sound.

One can make individual word banks for topic work by listing the words likely to be needed. These can be colour-coded and sound can be added. One can also use this feature for teaching particular sounds and reading and spelling practice, to suit the needs of the student.

For those students who would spend considerable time finding picture files and thus lose the thread of the work in hand, I place the graphics on to a disk, possibly according to their assignment, subject, or homework requirements. For younger children in a primary school, these would be done to support topic work. I load the graphics into Word, and save the files according to the topic itself. So I would have Egyptians 1 and 2 and Victorians 1, 2 and 3. I clearly label the disks and can then locate them when needed. I work in more than one school and I colour-code the disks per school according to the uniform. That way I know which disks belong where.

In order to add the graphics the pupil selects Open File from the File option in the menu bar and goes to Drive A, or wherever the floppy disk is inserted. When the file opens, the pupil highlights the picture required by clicking with the mouse and dragging the mouse over it, or just clicking so that it is highlighted, and selecting Copy from the toolbar. The copy icon looks like two sheets of paper. They then click on the document they are working on and paste, by clicking on the paste icon.

Each word-processor accomplishes this in a different way and you may have to resort to using a manual to find the precise technique required. Some word-processors are more user-friendly than others, so it is worth investing in a good manual and one that has clear, helpful illustrations.

Curriculum example

- Make a template of a newspaper as in Figure 6.7. This can include the font and size for the heading, the number of columns, boxes for pictures and so on. Different versions of Word and other word-processing software packages have different ways of achieving this, so it may be necessary to refer to the manual.
- Graphics can be added to these templates and stationery pads. So for MFL, or science, one can add suitable graphics to improve the presentation of the document.
- Recorded sound can be added to the templates and stationery pads at any time to act as an aide-memoire.

Figure 6.7 A newspaper template

Summary

Word-processors are very powerful tools especially given that they are present on most systems. Although not marketed for dyslexic pupils, with creative adaptation they are a very effective means of support.

Chapter 7

Facilities to aid word-processing

This chapter discusses software additions to complement a standard word-processor. They run alongside the word-processing program and the more powerful can be used with software other than word-processors.

I have already referred to Co-Writer which can be used with any word-processing package on either a PC or Apple computer. Co-Writer is a facility to aid word-processing.

TextHELP Read and Write (TextHELP Systems)

TextHELP was specifically designed for dyslexic students. It is an invaluable tool and is available for both PC and Apple computers. TextHELP can read text aloud and help construct words and sentences using word prediction. It has a talking spell-checker specifically designed for the dyslexic person, and a built-in screen-reader.

When TextHELP is open, an animated character is shown on-screen that will read the text aloud. There is the choice of four characters, of which Merlin is my favourite. If one prefers to have no animated character on the screen, the option can be switched off. There are eight voices to choose from, two of which are female.

The prediction function offers the words likely to be needed and TextHELP adapts to the vocabulary that a particular user favours. The spell-checker logs the number of spelling errors in a file, so you can see if your spelling is improving. Fourteen hundred commonly confused words are stored in TextHELP, along with their meanings. The program will speak the meaning of these words for the dyslexic pupil. Its features include:

- the ability to read aloud anything on the screen including, if you wish, menus, icons and functions;
- a 180,000 word dictionary;
- a spell-checker tailored to dyslexic errors;
- logging number of errors onto a file;
- automatic correction facility for dyslexic pupils;
- a separate database of homonyms;

- the ability to add or delete words;
- a prediction panel that can be customised with font, size, colour, etc.;
- a choice of voices; and
- a thesaurus.

A very important feature is its ability to read any text on the current computer screen. This facility means that dyslexic students can hear all the words displayed on the screen. My students have surfed the web and found the topic that they wanted, but then struggled to read the text. A considerable amount of information, such as research papers, is available on the web and enabling access to it will become increasingly important. Dyslexic students might wish to email their friends, and they need to double-check what they have written. When they receive a reply, they cannot always read it. Access to all of this is denied to some dyslexic students who cannot read the documents, especially as the reading age of some of this material is at an adult level. This software assists the pupils by vocalising the content. It empowers the dyslexic student to access finding information and enhances their study skills at one stroke.

It is very likely that soon most books will be published with a CD-ROM included so that the entire book can be read from a computer.

The voice is robotic and therefore aids spelling for the reasons described in Chapter 5. The ending of the words is very clear and the student can better hear what is being said. The speech is also slower than normal speech and this is helpful for the slower phonological processing skills of most dyslexics.

TextHELP also supports French, as well as working alongside Voice Activated Software (VAS) which will be discussed in Chapter 8. TextHELP is proving to be a very useful piece of software.

Concept keyboards

On both Apple and PC machines one can attach a large touch-sensitive pad typified by the term concept keyboard. In its simplest use the teacher, helper or parent decides what they wish the pupil to do and designs the **overlay** that rests on the keyboard. Concept keyboards either replace the traditional keyboard as an input device, or work alongside it. One normally has to purchase software that will support the concept keyboard.

The concept keyboard consists of 128 cells called a **grid**. Each cell can contain a letter, word, phrase, sentence or command. When pressed, the contents of the cell are inserted into the software being used, or the command is carried out. These keyboards are useful when linked to databases, for the children can insert information fast. The process of looking at the database and searching it can be done quickly. These concept keyboards are now seen in a slightly different format at the checkout tills of most supermarkets, or in restaurants where the operators touch a **cell** and the bill is automatically customised and totalled.

In education, these keyboards were used for a few years, and some are still in existence, but they have mostly been replaced by on-screen keyboards.

Clicker 4 (Crick Software) and Discover (Don Johnston)

Clicker 4 and Discover are two examples of on-screen keyboards. These are virtual keyboards, or keyboard emulators. The software is loaded and left running until needed by particular children, such as when dyslexic pupils feel they need that facility. To describe what Clicker 4 does, the following is a quote from the manual:

> Clicker 4 is an on-screen tool that allows you to do many things at the click of a mouse.

> The Clicker 4 window, called a **grid**, is divided up into cells. Each cell will normally contain a letter, word, phrase or picture and, when you click on it, can perform one or more of the following actions:

> - enter text into your word-processor or any other application;
> - output software speech;
> - output a sound sample;
> - perform the action of an editing or function key such as Delete;
> - close the current grid and open a new one;
> - start another software application.

> Clicker 4 grids can be any size and can take any position on your screen. Cells too can also be any size and can use any font or colour.

> A key feature of Clicker 4 is its ease of use. You can change both the contents and the action of any cell at any time and the effect is instant – you do not have to get into the complications of a set-up program.

Discover will also do all of this – with the additional benefit, for those pupils requiring greater physical access features, of having a separate board that connects to the computer. This totally replaces the keyboard and thus gives greater control for the pupil, although this extra functionality is quite expensive.

With both of these pieces of software, one can create specific word banks, although both do already have considerable resources pre-written and supplied with the package. These can be customised, or you can create your own. Consequently, pupils can have a simplified keyboard on the screen and can select the desired cell only and have its contents inserted into the software being used. Alternatively, they can have banks of words, or sentences, such as for a specific subject, and can select their choice. The individual word, or sentence, is then inserted into the document. Younger children can quickly enter data into a spreadsheet or database.

Uses of Clicker 4 and Discover

My younger students have used this software to help with story-writing and with topic work. The words for the topic can be entered into the software and selected as required. Part sentences can be included to help with writing.

My younger pupils have also used it to enter data into a traffic survey that they were conducting. My older students have used this facility for writing CVs and letters of application. Other older students have used it for subject-specific work, where difficult words were entered to help them, particularly in subjects like science.

Draft:Builder (Don Johnston)

Draft:Builder is an organisational/planning tool which also supports the writing process, and it was specifically designed for struggling writers, including dyslexic students. Draft:Builder has various sections beginning with *Outlining and Mapping*. In this section there is a dynamic connection between the outline and the visual map, which helps the pupil to build a framework for writing which includes the main and also supporting ideas. While supporting the pupil through this planning process, the software also helps the student acquire the organisational skills necessary for future writing. The next section is *Taking Notes*, which is an area where the students can develop their ideas and thoughts further, by adding notes for each sub-topic. Moving and reorganising the notes is easy, so that the student is very much in control of the whole process. From this section the student moves to *Building a Draft* where the outline and notes are integrated so that the students can easily build a logically sequenced draft. This draft can be exported to any word-processor, where finishing touches, including graphics, can be added. Draft:Builder has a built-in Franklin spell-checker with speech and there are teacher-made as well as standard templates which help pupils to write in different genres. This software is particularly suitable for students aged from 9 years to adult.

Writer's Toolkit, SCET (TAG)

Writer's Toolkit is helpful for some dyslexic students. It takes the student step-by-step through the process of writing. The student chooses the type of writing he or she wishes to produce, from the choices of Imaginative, Personal or Functional. The student is guided through the individual processes required by that type of writing. Help is on hand for those who need it by clicking on the different icons on the screen and, as the student progresses through the software, further facilities are added. The steps are progressive and are finally added to a document from which the spelling can be checked and final editing occur. For students who need structure in writing, this has proved a useful thinking tool, and one that is supportive, particularly for pupils from the top of the junior age range, through to GCSE.

Summary

We know word-processing is powerful in helping dyslexic pupils and word-processors in their own right are a good tool. If we sensibly select a complementary package greater results can be achieved.

Chapter 8

Industry standard software 2: linked specifically to the National Curriculum

Writing skills are an important target; however, ICT provides a much larger range of access capability. In this chapter we will look at other packages which offer access to all of the NC especially when used in conjunction with word-processing.

Spreadsheets

A spreadsheet is a grid, consisting of rows and columns. Think of a register in a school and it looks a bit like that, except that one cannot see all of it at once because the grid is often very large. Consequently one usually sees only a section, the size of which will depend on the size of the screen on your computer. However, unlike a grid in a register book, it can have mathematical formulae and functions included in it. So it will, if told to, add up automatically all the numbers in one column. It can also give an average if required. The calculations requested can be quite basic, or they can be very complicated. One can even have multiple worksheets within one spreadsheet, the equivalent of a book of registers.

Spreadsheets are used throughout industry and are used by universities and research departments. Before one becomes a little intimidated, they can also, once suitably customised, be used by KS1 pupils. The advantages of using spreadsheets for dyslexic students are that:

- the numbers are automatically entered correctly orientated, i.e. facing the correct direction;
- the calculations are done accurately with no careless errors due to misreading the symbols, e.g. mistaking a + and x, an easy thing for a dyslexic pupil;
- the spreadsheet does the mechanics, leaving the student free to work on the job in hand, thus giving them access to the curriculum being taught; they are not hindered by the calculations and the volume of data, which can confuse;
- a spreadsheet allows different values to be inserted to test a hypothesis, e.g. one can ask what will be the effect on the profit, if the demand for a product decreases, or what happens if the demand increases;

- once the data is entered, it can be manipulated in different ways without having to re-enter the data; hence different hypotheses can be tested on the same data for far less effort than manual techniques;
- when the data is altered in any way, the student can immediately see all the other numbers that are affected and note the results;
- one can obtain a forecast from the data entered, so one could look at a set of figures and then get the spreadsheet to extrapolate the forecast;
- the charts section allows for a visible, easy-to-interpret representation of the data.

Spreadsheets can be constructed by the parent or teacher, so that they can perform all of the above functions but at a level appropriate for the student concerned. Alternatively, older students can design the spreadsheet themselves and enter the formulae. For the latter, it is necessary that the student understands the formulae and the mathematical concepts. Most dyslexic students are able to cope with this. The biggest drawback of spreadsheets is that people can trust them too much and, if there is a slight error in one of the cells, the results can be disastrous. Hence it is essential that programming the formulae into the cells is done very carefully, in a structured manner and is thoroughly tested before being relied upon.

When the data is entered and processed it can be displayed on a graph. Spreadsheets have a charts section, which will present the data graph in two- or three-dimensional format. There are many different types of charts available. The students soon learn to customise these according to their needs. This can be done for younger pupils by the parent or teacher. The chart can be visible at the same time as the data is displayed on the screen. As one alters the data in the cells, the chart automatically changes at the same time. This visual presentation of the data in graphical form is ideal for dyslexic pupils, for they can see at a glance the effects of changing the data.

Spreadsheets can also work like a database allowing the usual save, sort and search facilities.

A good introduction to spreadsheets and to learn the environment is a piece of software called The Cruncher (REM). This consists of many customised spreadsheets that can be changed or used directly from the program.

How spreadsheets can support access to the curriculum

- Spreadsheets are obviously useful for mathematics, particularly statistics for the older student. For the younger student they can be customised to look like magic squares. This is where the numbers in each line in a grid add up to the same total.
- Teachers can design their own spreadsheets to suit the curriculum needs. Parents can design them to suit different purposes, such as to calculate pocket money, or chores done around the house.
- In humanities (history and geography) spreadsheets are very useful. They will hold data for activities such as traffic surveys, population trends, dates of famous battles, reigns of kings and queens, etc.

- They will process and sort any data required, so one can compare different rivers by their length, or the depth of the oceans, etc.
- Weather data can be analysed, e.g. frequency of sunny days, average rainfall, wind direction, etc.
- One group I have recently worked with placed lots of census material on to a spreadsheet. This was then searched for different aspects of the population. The students wished to know how many children there were compared to how many adults and so on. Census information from different years was compared and plotted on graphs.
- Science is another subject area where spreadsheets are useful. Again they hold the data and provide interesting graphs. For biology, the pupils can plot the growth of plants under different conditions; for chemistry, temperature variations as liquid boils; for physics, extension of springs under different loadings.
- Sensing equipment can provide data about soil, temperature, humidity and so on. This can be entered into a spreadsheet and then subsequently plotted on to graphs.

This kind of data would take too long to manage by hand, but a spreadsheet can do the required calculations, sifting and sorting, etc., in a matter of seconds.

Claris Works and Microsoft Works

Claris Works, Microsoft Works, Textease Studio are integrated packages that offer word-processing, a database and a spreadsheet. Compared to Microsoft Office, they have reduced functionality; however, they offer an economic method of delivering a great deal of ICT NC capability and, like their bigger brothers, both are industry standard software.

For Apple users, Claris Works is often provided in the purchase price of the computer. Computer hardware is relatively cheap to buy; much of the cost of a computer system relates to the price of the software installed on the machine. To reduce the purchase cost of a computer, the supplier will supply a cheaper integrated software package, like these two, rather than complete packages such as Microsoft Office.

Claris Works is widely used in primary schools, particularly among those who use Apples. It is also available for PC use. Claris Works is easy to customise and TAG sell templates ready to use, which can save teachers and parents a lot of time. These templates are particularly customised for the primary curriculum, although some Y7 groups, aged 11–12, would also find them useful.

The word-processing part of Claris suffices, although it will not, to my knowledge, take sound. It also has desktop publishing facilities (in Claris Works) which enabled one junior school to produce their termly newsletter and these features are often useful for older pupils. There is also a graphics section.

Generally, these types of integrated packages represent reasonable value for money and provide enough facilities to meet the needs of many students up to the completion of their school careers. I know of one self-employed businesswoman who uses Microsoft Works for all of her business needs, and finds it perfectly adequate.

Example of using Claris Works and Microsoft Works

One infant group had been growing cress and they needed to work out the results of the different growing media, with graphs to illustrate their findings. The data was entered into Claris Works and plotted on a graph. As these were young children the template was designed so that the data and the graph were displayed on the monitor together as in Figure 8.1. The class readily entered the data and enjoyed manipulating it while discussing and interpreting the results.

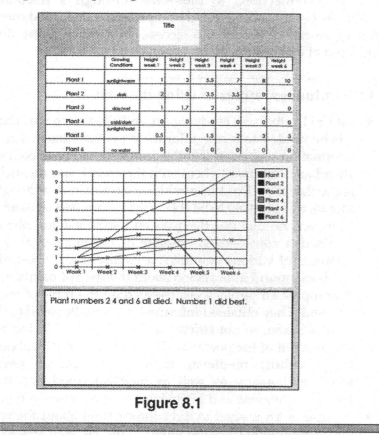

Figure 8.1

Internet browsing software

Two of the most common Internet browsers are Netscape Communicator and Microsoft Internet Explorer. An important component of the Internet is the World Wide Web, or web for short. Exploring the web is sometimes referred to as **surfing**. By exploring the web one can access an enormous amount of information, including the latest research. My pupils love using the web and use it to facilitate their work. One word of caution for parents: using the web is via the telephone line and so is not free. It requires an ISP (Internet Service Provider, e.g. Demon, Compuserve, AOL, Freeserve, etc.). However, there are a number of low-cost solutions available. The fundamental difference between ISPs is whether they charge a monthly fee for the service. Many ISPs, such as AOL and Compuserve, charge a monthly subscription fee. They may offer the first month of surfing for free, but ultimately they will charge. They often offer their own versions of web-browsing software and email packages. This has the advantage of saving you having to locate such software, but has the disadvantage of often not being consistent with other web-browsing software. Companies such as Freeserve do not charge monthly subscription fees, but generate their income through the cost of the telephone calls. They do not often offer the 'complete package' approach of companies such as AOL, but instead, they typically use third party software such as MSIE or Netscape. There is a third option for parents living in most major towns, which is access through cable TV connections. This is often very quick, but also more expensive. However, connections to the www through a telephone will eventually become obsolete and be replaced by dedicated connections offering so-called 'broadband' access, with much faster download times, but at a premium.

Curriculum examples of using the web

- One Y11 pupil was studying art and the theme was time. For this he needed to access information about Monet. The GCSE information suggested that the pupils should be encouraged to attend an exhibition to help with their work and research. This particular pupil lived in rural Lincolnshire and, although near a town, was unlikely to be able to attend any Monet exhibitions. However, he did use the web and searched for Monet. He obtained a considerable amount of information along with printouts of various paintings, a picture of the artist himself, and background information about the style of painting.
- A group of Y6 pupils were researching the topic of medieval England. They obtained information about Beowulf (although he was Saxon, so not strictly speaking medieval), including a full printout of the poem; medieval castles; medieval clothing; King Arthur; medieval monsters; medieval jewellery; medieval housing as well as medieval food and hygiene (medieval hygiene and manners were most interesting).
- A pupil in Y8 wished to have information about the weather for an assignment he was working on. He was able to locate the area in question, California, and acquire the latest weather information from two different satellites, and produce printouts.

Dyslexic pupils are often reluctant to use libraries. Even at KS2, pupils are expected to be able to research their own information. Without the full complement of required study skills, any pupil is disadvantaged. However, dyslexic pupils will readily use the web, for it does not depend upon knowing alphabetical order.

If the pupil cannot read what is on the screen then TextHELP will help by reading the words.

Once the topic has been researched and the required information found, the student can save the information to disk for use in a future assignment. This can include pictures.

If one has a modem, one can also send and receive emails. These are electronic messages sent via the telephone line. One needs to have a service provider to be able to send emails.

Once the facility is available, one is given an email address. Email is fast, messages are sent in a matter of seconds, and it is cheaper than ordinary land mail, sometimes referred to as 'snail mail', to distinguish it from its electronic counterpart.

Usually email is charged at local telephone rates. It means that one can write to relatives in Australia, or anywhere else in the world, for a very small cost. Pupils can use this to contact penfriends living anywhere in the world providing those penfriends have access to email.

Special cautions regarding dyslexic pupils' use of email

Perhaps more than most of the other aspects of ICT that have been so far covered in this book, the use of email presents particular problems for dyslexic pupils. It is vital to bear in mind that because the transmission of email is so fast – just the click of a mouse – sending a message before it is ready to be sent can easily leave the dyslexic child feeling vulnerable: they do not have the normal safeguards that exist in traditional letter-writing and this can cause them to feel embarrassed and humiliated if, as is much more likely to happen than with private 'snail mail', their message is forwarded to someone who doesn't know them – and before it is actually ready to be sent.

VAS is receiving a great deal of publicity and appears to be a wonderful and exciting facility. However, as with all developments, there are teething problems. VAS is the ability to speak into a microphone and see the text appear on the screen as one speaks. This type of software is not new, but has been slowly evolving over a number of years and I believe that the education specialists in this area are Father Alan Cotgrove (BDACC) and the company iANSYS.

Ideally, this should be a perfect answer for most dyslexic pupils, for they should be able to sit in front of a computer, speak, and the text, correctly spelt, will appear on the screen.

It is essential that one advises the user to check the specifications for the computer system required very carefully. For instance, Alan has written: 'A duplex sound card is needed for nearly all VAS systems, but cards called duplex are not all ideal. Those which are only partially duplex can cause time delays with the speech. Care must be taken here. Even the quality of the microphone matters. Be prepared for this.'

Whatever the specification stated on the VAS software for the memory and speed of the computer, that will be an absolute minimum and one will really need a more powerful machine than stated, if one wishes to use this software effectively.

VAS software was designed for adult males and is more suited to the adult male voice. Problems can be experienced with young children and female voices. This can cause obvious difficulties for adolescent males with their voices changing. Speech difficulties, e.g. unusual accents or indistinct speech also can cause complications.

Users need to be able to read the words on the screen so that they can check what is being written. Alan also feels that they must be able to speak and think clearly, be able to read and have editing skills.

For students over about 15 years of age, particularly for male students, VAS is a possible option. However, VAS, at this point in time, does not appear to be very suitable for use in a school environment for many reasons. And although VAS is available for other languages, it requires a new purchase to be made for each language which can prove expensive.

Summary

The predominance of industry standard software, such as Microsoft Office (in particular Word and Excel), with access to the web and email, gives students the added advantage that they are already familiar with the software most likely to be used when they leave school, either at university, or where they will work. They understand the jargon and the language being used.

Chapter 9

Logo and Control

As a subject, learning mathematics can be likened to learning a foreign language. It has its own specific vocabulary, grammar and syntax. Consequently it presents difficulties for dyslexic students. Many numeracy schemes require a considerable amount of reading. The printed page can be cluttered and have very small printed mathematical symbols. In addition the reading level of the text is often quite advanced. All of these issues present barriers that can stop the dyslexic student accessing mathematics.

The language of mathematics is confusing. I spent one session of about an hour teaching a group of 5-year-olds about fractions. We concentrated on halves and quarters. I felt that they had understood the concepts after cutting cakes, dividing chocolate beans, cutting paper and so on.

The following week I went to work again with this group and I always begin each lesson with a Newsround session, when each child practises their speaking and listening skills, by giving one piece of news about something they have enjoyed during the week.

One little girl in this group promptly said, 'My sister has a new boyfriend and he is only *half* a boyfriend.'

Feeling rather confused I asked her what she meant by him being 'only half a boyfriend'.

My expression must have reflected my disbelief, for she replied, 'Well, my daddy says that this boyfriend is like her other boyfriend, and he is not all there!'

I have personally found that my dyslexic pupils like to work from a practical base, using suitable mathematical equipment. For mathematics, as with most subjects, there is no substitute for a good teacher. However, ICT NC does support a considerable number of mathematical skills. Spreadsheets, mentioned in Chapter 8, are one obvious example. Other areas include Logo and Control.

Logo

Logo is a requirement of the National Curriculum both for ICT and mathematics. Logo is a programming language used to control a **turtle,** or floor robot. The turtle is displayed on the screen and the program allows the student to issue directions for the turtle to follow. These commands can be relatively simple, such as 'move forward', or they can be quite complex. The instructions are written as a set of specific commands, using the special programming language provided. This is almost like formal computer programming and really requires the same logical approach to the task. If the turtle on the screen is also linked to a physical robot, this constitutes **computer control**. The commands are entered into the computer, which in turn controls the robot.

By doing these tasks the student learns about measurement, estimation, geometry, direction and so on. Most dyslexic students find this an environment that they enjoy for it is based on logic and problem solving. They find it stimulating and they can participate in problem solving activities. The instructions are written as procedures and these require the student to remember sequences of commands/instructions, which exercises their organisational skills and also their short-term memory. This type of software encourages logical thought processes.

Roamer (Valiant Technology)

A Roamer is a circular robot that can be programmed. This is now available with Windows Software. It is often used in conjunction with Logo as a first contact with the language. If the Roamer's plain appearance is not stimulating, one can purchase covers for it and the Roamer can be made to look like a large bumblebee, ladybird or other such design. The programming section is in the centre of the Roamer. The Roamer can be made to move in any direction, with steps that can be customised in length. It can rotate in varying angles and even make noises.

When programming the Roamer, the short-term memories of the students are constantly being used and extended, as are their logic, problem solving and sequencing skills. This can all be in a fun and creative environment, according to how the task is designed.

An example of using a Roamer

One can have seven pieces of card that are shaped like sheep, each with the word of one day of the week printed on them. These sheep can be placed on the floor in any order. The pupil can send the Roamer to the sheep with Monday on it, followed by finding Tuesday and so on. Maps on the floor can be drawn with specific routes that the Roamer must follow. There are many ways of using this type of device. If a Roamer is not available any programmable robot will be useful.

The only difficulties with this type of robot are:

1. the batteries, which need recharging and are fairly expensive to buy; and
2. the length of the cables, if they are attached to the mains and to a computer, which can be limiting.

First Logo, *Longman Logotron* (TAG)

First Logo is a simplified version of Logo and is particularly suitable for young children. It serves as a good introduction to the Logo language. The Turtle on the screen can be customised to represent an animal and children find this entertaining. The software also comes with a good booklet with clear instructions.

Turtle Maths, *LCSI* (TAG)

As children get older, they can progress to more advanced software such as Turtle Maths, LCSI (TAG). Turtle Maths has eight areas of activities. The children learn about geometry, logic and problem solving. This software is suitable for children in KS2 and KS3. The activities are well constructed and designed. Suggested Turtle Maths investigations include probability, patterns, geometry, computing and similarity, along with problem solving and logic skills. There are good support materials that can be used by both parents and teachers.

The Crystal Rain Forest, *Sherston* (REM)

The Crystal Rain Forest program is presented in the format of an adventure game and involves lots of direction finding, use of Logo and estimation. In this program, the pupils have the task of finding or making magic crystals to save the Rain Forest. This software is suitable for KS2 and 3 pupils for use at home or in school.

From here the pupil progresses to programs such as WinLogo (Longman Logotron). This is really for KS3/4 and preferably for pupils with some previous experience of Logo. Dyslexic students readily take to Logo and enjoy using it. At the same time, it helps their short-term memory and organisational, as well as directional, skills.

The subject Control is a requirement of ICT NC. Control involves looking at technology which is currently available in society, such as burglar alarms and sensors, and getting the student to use the technology for simulations, designing their own systems and solutions to given problems.

Control (various software available from REM such as Junior Control Insight and Control Insight)

Examples of using Control

- Some students might look at the design of burglar alarms and link them to sensors.
- Others might look at traffic lights or warning lights at level crossings etc. and design systems for coping with the circumstances represented.
- Using computer control the students might be required to design a system for detecting and calculating the number of cars entering a theme park via its many entrances, in order to ensure that overcrowding does not occur.

> **Further curriculum examples for Control**
>
> - Junior school pupils designed and built a greenhouse. They constructed it out of cheap wood, placed polythene over the frame and then added a door and window. The soil was placed in trays and seeds planted. The children had to place sensors for humidity and temperature within the greenhouse. Specific parameters were given to the computer and, if the soil was too dry, or if the temperature either fell or rose, then an alarm would sound.
> - The same school planned to use a large ramp that had a light sensor at the top and one at the bottom. Cars were allowed to travel down the ramp and the computer measured the time for the car to reach the lower sensor. Using the time measured and keeping the distance travelled constant by using the same start and end positions, the best car design could be determined. The results of the above experiments could be placed on to a spreadsheet and analysed if one wished.

When using Control, it might be necessary to use a 'buffer box' that will enable the computer and the sensors to communicate.

Mapping ICT into the curriculum

Importantly, the National Curriculum in all subjects cross-references with ICT NC. This means that if one views each subject as a distinct vertical column, ICT is a horizontal strand that runs across all of them. ICT is ideally suited to meet the needs of dyslexic students. Every time ICT is used within a NC subject, there is a good chance that it is enabling access to that subject for the dyslexic student. It might be useful for parents to be able to cross-reference the types of software that support their child in the different subjects.

The following list might help:

Science:	Word-processing (WP) – art software – subject-specific software, spreadsheets and the web
Geography:	WP – art software – subject-specific software, spreadsheets and the web
History:	WP – art software – subject-specific software, spreadsheets and the web
Art:	WP – art software – subject-specific software and the web
English:	WP – art software – subject-specific software, spreadsheets, email and the web
Maths:	WP – subject-specific software, spreadsheets, web, Logo and Control
Technology:	WP – spreadsheets, Logo, Control, subject-specific software, CD-ROM, web
MFL:	WP (foreign fonts) – art software – CD-ROM – subject-specific software, spreadsheets and the web
Music:	WP – subject-specific software, electronic keyboards and the web

PE: WP – subject-specific software and sensors, such as pulse and blood pressure

It is of note that word-processing and subject-specific software occur in all of the above.

If we take an example of a subject such as an MFL, e.g. French, ICT support could begin with using cassette recorders and hand-held spell-checkers. Along with this, one could also use word-processors using foreign fonts, e.g. Word. Alternatively, one might use a talking word-processor, such as WriteOutloud. Co-Writer or TextHELP would provide additional functionality to Word, so that most dyslexic students would be able to access written text. If the teacher wished to create help/vocabulary files for the students, including recorded sound, these could be inserted into Word.

Art software could be used in the ways suggested in Chapter 4, including making talking books. Kid Pix Studio has an option to change into a French version, with appropriate labels. Subject-specific software is available and often includes large sections of the standard syllabus taught in many schools. One can also use the web to obtain information about France and email enables swift communication with penfriends.

Summary

By using the ideas in this and previous chapters, it is possible to support dyslexic students with ICT in virtually every single subject and at each key stage. ICT provides practice for the cognitive areas that are the weakest in dyslexic students, namely short-term memory, sequencing, spelling and reading, while pulling on their specific strengths. When dyslexic students use this software they are working on the same programs as their peers and so retain peer equality. At no time are they being labelled by working on different software. The software might be customised to meet their particular needs, but it is still the same software.

Chapter 10

Other software for the dyslexic student

A parent or a teacher wishing to purchase specific software for their dyslexic pupils/children can be confronted by a range of programs, each claiming to be an answer to the problems caused by dyslexia. An adult might have seen a particular piece of software demonstrated or have attended a course to hear specific virtues stressed and, understandably, they might deem that software to be a panacea. Indeed, clever marketing, often delivered by professionals, can be very persuasive. Parents in particular are in a difficult position. They are desperate to help their child. If someone makes promises about some software, it is understandable that they latch on to that and want it to solve their problems and those of their child. One can easily empathise and understand, for I have been in this position. The wider picture of ICT in school does not usually enter into the equation and the practical problems and organisation required for using the new, and different, software package are not always considered.

Software developers, who do not necessarily understand the mainstream education market and who, consequently, are not very knowledgeable about ICT in the education system, write most of the specific programs for dyslexic students. The software is often marketed with some sales stratagem, so that to use it one must attend a course, or buy a certain number of copies. Parents and teachers have no independent body to go to for advice, other than the BDACC.

It is difficult to set criteria for one to judge new software by, but you should check that:

- it is interesting and exciting;
- it is not opprobrious, insulting or patronising;
- it does not contain derogatory noises if the child gets something wrong;
- it does not merely cover the negative aspects of being dyslexic (for this reason I very rarely use spelling programs – these merely emphasise the detrimental aspects of being dyslexic and I have yet to see any raise the standards of spelling in any pupil; the only one I occasionally use is Word Shark, see p. 73);

- the software is useful for the rest of the peer group, so that the dyslexic student is not labelled as being different;
- it should not be a means to an end in itself, but grow with the student as they become more proficient;
- it must have the appropriate reading level of the pupil;
- it must have an age appropriate context.

In the past, parents and teachers have recommended particular pieces of software and when I evaluated them I found that the students were working away quite happily, but not necessarily in the way the parents and teachers thought. Some students found it more interesting to get the activities wrong, in order to find out what happened as a result. Other students would work happily at the computer to avoid doing other work, so were not learning, although appearing to be occupied. One spelling program was most interesting. If the student got the word wrong, a cloud entered the screen and from that cloud, a magical hand (a bit like the National Lottery advert) took hold of the wrong letters and crunched them up. Then a finger pointed to the correct choice and inserted it. If, however, the student got the word correct they got no reward at all, merely having to spell the next word. Much better to get it wrong, and you spent longer on the computer!

Some other students were telling me that they never got a question correct for either mathematics or spelling, because they said that they were always given a choice of three answers on software. If they were not correct on the third attempt, the computer invariably gave them the answer and so why bother? Some software is designed unintentionally, but nevertheless ideally, for the student who likes to guess. Dyslexics are good at guessing and enjoy this. Using software, therefore, needs very careful observation and teaching.

There is so much software on the market that it is only possible to mention a few programs. For additional programs the following catalogues are useful: REM, TAG, AVP and Don Johnston. Rather than produce a catalogue, or replicate one, I have chosen examples of software that I know are useful and suitable to use. How they have proved useful is also discussed, so that the types of programs should serve as a guide to parents and teachers in choosing other software. I also describe a few pitfalls to be aware of when viewing software.

If software caters for the dyslexic pupil and their particular skills, delivers some ICT NC capability as well as giving access to other NC subjects, then it is ideal to use. The software already mentioned in Chapters 4–9 does all of this.

Software designed specifically for dyslexic pupils

When discussing software options with teachers or parents, some do request specific software. The first area that I am usually asked about is spelling. The only spelling program that I would use is Word Shark.

Word Shark 3 (White Space)

Word Shark provides lots of practice for students who are struggling with spelling. The activities resemble games and the teacher can select the phonics to be practised as the student performs the activities. The environment is interesting, colourful and entertaining, with a choice of 36 games. The phonics are those in the scheme Alpha to Omega. Many parents and specialist teachers use this scheme of work. Therefore, Word Shark provides a way of consolidating the specific lesson that has been taught, by reinforcing the phonics learned. It can be used by teachers' aides and other supportive assistants, as well as the students themselves, who can decide which phonics are to be revised.

The Literacy Hour is now a part of most primary schools' curriculum, where the pupils learn various aspects of literacy including phonics. The latest version of Word Shark has all of the phonics of the Literacy Hour and one can easily switch between the Alpha to Omega section and the Literacy Hour part. The word lists can be printed off, to work with later, for further consolidation.

Number Shark (White Space)

Number Shark, as the name implies, is from the same software house as Word Shark, but focuses on supporting mathematics rather than English. The activities in Number Shark cover the four rules of number in very different ways. The teacher or parent decides the level of difficulty for the student to work at. The student can then choose from a wide range of different activities and various games to play. These vary considerably. The screen representing the main menu looks terribly cluttered and this can deter some people from using it. However, the students generally have no such problem and they often thoroughly enjoy using this software. It gives a score as they work and they often ask if they can have another turn in order to beat their previous total. This software is especially designed for dyslexic students and covers their specific needs. The only negative aspect is that it does produce an auditory noise when the student gets some things wrong and, therefore, I often turn the sound off. However, the environment is interesting, challenging and entertaining.

Both Word Shark and Number Shark are suitable for pupils aged 6–16 years.

Earobics (Don Johnston)

Earobics caters specifically for auditory development and phonics work. It consists of a series of games that are friendly and entertaining, based on scientific research and principles. The games include:

- Caterpillar Connection: for syllable and phoneme synthesis, auditory attention and memory;
- Basket Full of Eggs: for auditory discrimination, attention and memory;
- The C.C. Coal Car Train: for sound-symbol correspondence, recognition of sound and sound position in word, phonemic identification and discrimination;
- Rap-A-Tap-Tap: for auditory, syllable and phoneme segmentation, attention and memory;

- Rhyme Time: for rhyming, auditory figure-ground discrimination, attention and memory;
- Karloon's Balloons: for auditory memory, auditory and phoneme identification, discrimination and figure-ground discrimination and attention.

This software is relatively new to me, although already being used on a daily basis by some students. This program caters for students aged 4–7 (step one) and 7–11 years (step two).

Text-handling software

Programs that have a text facility, but not all of the options of a full word-processor, are referred to as text-handling software. Any software that allows text to be used is always useful for dyslexic students, and there are many types of this software around such as the following.

Easy Book, *Sunburst* (REM)

Easy Book is suitable for KS1–2. It is in a page format, with a picture facility at the top of the page and a text facility at the bottom of the page (see Figure 10.1). The entire page is seen on the screen and the software is easy to use. The graphics facility is a little limited and the text option has no spell-checker. However, it can be used in conjunction with the hand-held Franklin spell-checker. A number of my pupils have enjoyed using this software.

Sometimes it is wet and the pitch is dangerous. When players get hurt they have to be carried off.

Mrttin cot the ball. He thohw it owt to the playh.

Figure 10.1 Work done by a 9-year-old pupil

Storybook Weaver Deluxe, *Learning Company* (REM)

Storybook Weaver (suitable for KS2–3) is a graphics and text environment where the graphics are predefined. These graphics consist of banks of icons that one pastes onto another bank of various screens. The children enjoy this software, but the production of the pictures can take an inordinately long time, resulting in little word-processing. One needs to be aware of this.

I used this software with a group of junior school children and I expected them just to create pictures with relatively little text. The girls in the group decided that the picture part 'got in the way' and they quickly found how to write a page without having any illustrations, so that their story would develop. Figure 10.2 shows their story, about the Vikings, which was the topic being taught in the primary school during that term. All of the pupils were dyslexic and the finished product was impressive. The children were particularly pleased with what they had achieved.

Having mentioned this software, I must add that if an adult is knowledgeable enough about Word, they can customise it via a template to do all that the above two pieces of software can, and with much more functionality.

The children left behind played a game. The girl and boy were playing chase while their mum's talked. The women were discussing the next meal and how worried they were about the explorers.

The weather was rough and the boat was tossed about on the waves. The viking raider's finally arrive at an unknown place. This was actually America, but they did not know.

Figure 10.2 Work done by a group of 9-year-old pupils

Software for younger children

The next few pieces of software are ideally suited for younger dyslexic pupils. They are all exciting, multimedia environments which are entertaining while being educational.

Granny's Garden, *4MATION* (REM)

Mike Matson originally wrote Granny's Garden for the old BBC computers in 1983. It proved so successful that it has subsequently been versioned for different types of machines. Children are transported into a world where they can use their own imaginations, while being in an educational environment. Granny's Garden is a cross-curricular piece of software, which stimulates many follow-up activities. Both parents and teachers can do these and the software comes with a resource pack with many useful suggestions.

Millie's Maths House, *Iona* (TAG)

Millie's Maths House has a very entertaining suite of rooms, representing Millie's House. In these rooms the children can perform various mathematical activities. Each room is fully equipped with sound and is interesting yet educational. This software is good for basic mathematical language development and basic concepts of mathematics. Pupils with whom I have used this have thoroughly enjoyed working on it.

Bailey's Book House, *Iona* (TAG)

Bailey's Book House is an environment where Bailey sits on his chair and one can click on different parts of his room to select different activities. These include rhyming and listening activities ideally suited to the dyslexic child. Interesting printouts can be obtained for follow-up work. This software is good for practising phonological processing skills.

Sammy's Science House, *Iona* (TAG)

One meets Sammy and can select science activities from the main screen. These are ideally suited to the dyslexic student. They include making a movie where pictures have to be placed in their correct order and then made into a film (see Figure 10.3). One can also select the weather in the Weather Machine and can watch the film of the chosen options. The children love this. This software is good for providing practice in placing things in sequential order and for the language of basic science.

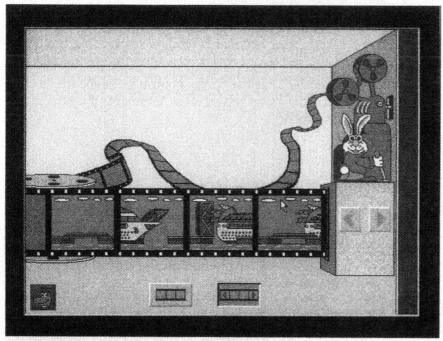

Figure 10.3 Making a movie in Sammy's Science House

Kid Desk, *Edmark* (REM)

Kid Desk is a facility to stop young children reaching the desktop of the Apple where they might be able to delete files. This software is not available for PCs as far as I know. Kid Desk can be customised to meet the special requirements of the children and looks like a desk of their own. It contains features such as a light, that can be switched off; a pencil case; a telephone, which can have messages recorded on to it (good for short-term memory and listening skills); a calendar, which is particularly pleasant in that it has a printout facility and one can enter special notes and dates, with a bank of picture icons to help. This facility is wonderful for the dyslexic student, for they can enter homework, or dates to remember, with clear printouts.

Kid Keys, *Davidson* (TAG)

Kid Keys is a multimedia program originally designed for children to become familiar with the Qwerty keyboard. However, I do not use it in that way, preferring instead to use it for learning initial sounds. For instance, on level one of the program, the pupil is asked 'to find the letter Q' and they have to press the correct letter. When they do this the letter Q changes to become a Queen. There are three different levels of difficulty. When the pupils complete the alphabet, they get a printout of a certificate of achievement. A great way to learn phoneme and grapheme correlation.

First Keys to Literacy, *Widget* (REM)

First Keys to Literacy links keyboard awareness with very early literacy skills. It comprises of nine activities, which range from letter recognition to spelling. These activities use pictures, speech and sound and so are multisensory. The pupil is learning the location of the letters on the computer keyboard, while also learning the letter sound (phoneme) and its shape (grapheme). If required, the software has stickers that can be attached to the computer keyboard, so that the pupil has exact matching between the letters on the screen and the letters on the keyboard.

Software for pupils aged seven upwards

Thinkin' Things 2 and 3, *Iona* (TAG)

Thinkin' Things 2 and 3 is an interesting suite of CD-ROMs. Thinking Things 2 has five activities. Three are ideally suited for dyslexic children and cover memory work, both auditory (Pelmanism) and visual (sequential), as well as phonological processing skills and auditory sequential memory.

Concentration is the first and this is the game of Pelmanism in a visual environment. The pupil has to match the pictures on the cards into pairs as shown in Figure 10.4. Unlike ordinary card games, there are levels of difficulty and a seemingly inexhaustible supply of games to play. The second part of this section is Pelmanism with sounds. The pictures on the cards are all the same, but each card has an individual sound and the pupils

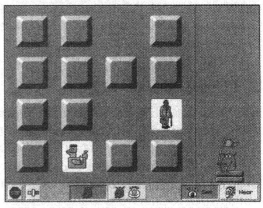

Figure 10.4 Concentration in Thinkin' Things 2

have to match the pairs. This area is ideally suited to the dyslexic student.

The second activity is **Looney Tunes**, which features a bird called Looney pictured in Figure 10.5. He has a glockenspiel and tunes to choose from. One can choose to learn a tune and Looney plays it in different parts. The pupil has to remember the notes and the order that they were played in. If the pupil gets it wrong, Looney helps them to relearn it. If they are correct, he shows them the next part. This can be great fun.

The third section is **Oranga and his band**. In this section, the pupils have to listen to tunes and say who played them. Alternatively, they can listen to tunes and click on the line played by one member of the group. Again there are levels of difficulty with many options. Great for auditory memory.

Figure 10.5 Looney Tunes in Thinkin' Things 2

The Logical Journey of the Zoombinis, *Broderbund* (TAG)

The Logical Journey of the Zoombinis is a challenging adventure game where the pupils have to solve mathematical problems in order to save the Zoombinis. The pupils enjoy the interface and the activities. It helps discussion and group work. This program has different levels of difficulty. Games of this type help the pupils enjoy mathematics, as well as problem solving activities.

Knowsley Woods, *Knowsley* (REM)

Knowsley Woods is designed to support Key Stage 2 mathematics, in particular levels 3–5 of NC. The scene is set in the eerie, but totally fictional world of Knowsley Woods. The pupils move through the wood, collecting waste materials, so improving the wood's natural environment. The pupils enjoyed using this software and found it to be motivating. Knowsley Woods is consistent with the goals and the lesson plans of the National Numeracy Strategy. There are some 23 games each with three levels of difficulty.

Maths Circus 1, 2 and 3 (4Mation)

Maths Circus consists of a suite of activities with five levels of difficulty, apart from Maths Circus 3, which has ten levels of difficulty. The puzzles are mathematical, as they require reasoning and the students enjoy attempting to solve them. The software is easy to use; covers many mathematical problems; has minimal screen text; records the progress of each student, which can easily be printed out; covers a wide range of skills. My students really do enjoy using this software and never seem to tire of it.

Games of Strategy (4Mation)

Games of Strategy is a challenging environment where there are 15 mathematical 'games'. There is a minimal amount of reading needed for students can quickly work out what is required and rarely need any instructions, preferring 'trial and error' techniques instead. Each 'game' has four levels of difficulty and there are some on-screen hints, although few students seem to use these. The pupil can play against another pupil, or against the computer, often declaring that the latter 'cheats'. There are printable worksheets on the CD-ROM and one can print a progress report for each student.

Start-to-Finish Books (Don Johnston)

Start-to-Finish Books were specifically written to encourage the older reader to become interested in reading. The titles include many 'classics' such as abridged versions of Shakespeare's 'Romeo and Juliet'. Each Start-to-Finish Book has a CD-ROM, a copy of the text in a book format and a cassette tape. The pages displayed on the monitor from the CD-ROM are exactly the same as the pages in the textbook and there is full supportive digital sound. As the page on the screen is being 'read' by the computer, the word, or sentence can be highlighted. I have found that some struggling readers, who were also unmotivated regarding reading books, have enjoyed using the Start-to-Finish Books and in so doing, have made considerable progress in their ability to read. Most importantly though, they have been encouraged to read other books.

Buildability (Don Johnston)

Buildability is an authoring program that enables the pupils to create multimedia presentations. Buildability is easy to use, but very complex to explain. It supports the students in expressing their comprehension, or ideas, by enabling them to create stories or presentations, which include animated drawings, graphics, text, speech and sounds. The speech and highlighted text link both written and spoken words. This software can be used for students of all key stages, as well as for teachers. I saw one teacher create an alphabet that was then animated. She formed the letters as they should be written and the software animated these. She then created a multimedia book, so that the pupils could see how to write and form the letters correctly. The pupils had their own section on each page, to attempt the writing process. The same teacher created a 'number book' where she drew the numbers, which were then animated, and placed animated dots alongside each number. The software allowed her to time the dots to have a one second interval between them, so that the pupil could count aloud while watching the number and the dots appear on the screen. All of these presentations can be printed and the pupil has his/her own customised book. Older students can readily create their own presentations for individual subjects, e.g. the water cycle.

CD-ROMs

There are various CD-ROMs available covering many topics connected with education. The following are subject-specific and are all available from REM:

- for Biology or Examination PE: *The Ultimate Human Body* (Dorling Kindersley);
- for Botany: *Botanical Gardens* (Sunburst);
- for Science: *Encyclopaedia of Science and Technology* and *Encyclopaedia of Nature* (Dorling Kindersley);
- for Science and Technology: *The Way Things Work 2* (Dorling Kindersley);
- for Geography: *Encarta 99 World Atlas* (Microsoft), *3D Atlas* (Electronic Arts), *World Reference Atlas* (Dorling Kindersley), *Where in the World is Carmen Sandiego?* (Broderbund) and *Weathermapper* (TAG);
- for History: *Britain Since the 1930s* (News Multimedia), *Victorian Britain* (News Multimedia), *Microsoft Ancient Lands* (Microsoft/TAG).
- For topic work, especially in KS2 although not exclusively so, some of the specific CD-ROMs currently available include:
  Vikings Anglia (REM)
  Life in Tudor Times (Chalksoft/REM)
  Castle Explorer (Dorling Kindersley/REM)
  Ancient Greeks (Anglia/REM)
  Romans (Anglia/REM)
  The Evacuees (4MATION)
  Betsi (*The Tudor Dog*) (4MATION)
  Athenian Life (4MATION)
  Journeys in the Roman Empire (British Museum Press/REM)
  How we used to Live: Early Victorians (Granada/REM)
  How we used to Live: Late Victorians (Granada/REM)

These are just a few of the many CD-ROMs available. Try to view them first and check that they are appropriate; however, remember that the dyslexic student will find them easy to navigate around. If the reading level is difficult, then TextHELP will read the screen to the student. From that screen, text can be saved onto a disk and then used as a quotation in assignments. Pupils from KS2 upward use this technology to great effect. The Appendix to this book contains addresses of software providers from whom CD-ROMs can be purchased.

Software to support study skills

Study skills are sometimes referred to as the process of learning and acquiring knowledge, as well as how to organise your study. Using Outline mode in Word enables students to view their work in an outline format, thus helping with organisation of the text. Some software is designed specifically for organisation purposes such as Inspiration (iANSYS), Wordswork (iANSYS), and Think Sheet (Fisher Marriott). Dyslexic students might find this type of software particularly useful, so try it and see if it helps. Please also refer to Draft:Builder, which has already been mentioned on page 59.

Integrated Learning Systems (ILS)

Integrated Learning Systems (ILS) are systems that are computer-based learning packages. They usually include:

- some kind of assessment of the pupil in order to inform the teacher where the pupil should be placed on the scheme;
- the pupil receiving computer-based lessons, which are aimed at the correct level for that particular student, following the assessment;
- an administration area that gives the teacher a printout of the achievements, or results, of each individual child either after each lesson or at regular intervals, e.g. weekly.

Lexia UK Reading System (Lexia Learning System Inc.)

Lexia UK Reading System is an ILS for students aged 7 to adult. Lexia is a reading program which reinforces the application of word attack strategies to single words and contextual materials. The Lexia Reading System provides five 'activities' where the students can enjoy using the phonics that they have learned and is a very structured system, which builds on the skills previously learned. The software provides a motivating and interesting environment which most students enjoy. Indeed, for some severely dyslexic students it has proved to be a very valued piece of supportive software, which they will readily use.

The Academy of Reading, *Autoskill International* (TAG)

The Academy of Reading is a multimedia, interactive reading program that develops basic to high-level reading skills, from phonemic awareness to reading comprehension. It is suitable for pupils from 4 years of age to adult, who have reading difficulties. Chris Johnston in an article in TES ONLINE, 8 January 1999, commented:

> At £2,750 for five users and £3,750 for 10 users, it is not cheap, but Julian Sibbald, head of learning support at Bournville Secondary School in Birmingham, is one who believes that the benefits of the software justify its cost...Julian Sibbald says the pupils clearly enjoyed using the software and stayed well motivated during the six-month trial. Most importantly, all of them significantly increased their reading accuracy and comprehension.

The article is very objective for it goes on to say:

> Although the program maintains pupils' attention well, Mr. Sibbald says that the teacher's role in motivating pupils is still important. 'It's certainly not just a plug in and play thing – the students have to be monitored very carefully.'

If an ILS system is available in the school, then it could prove useful.

If any software, or software use, is a replica of a paper-based system, then one should question the ICT usage. After all, computers are in short supply and expensive, so one must ask what advantages adding an ICT extension gives. The advantages have to be considerable to justify the use of a computer. If the system merely equates to the paper-based system, then use the latter.

In my opinion, it is an incorrect use of ICT merely to do skills and drills work. It is for this reason that I very rarely use spelling or reading programs. If one wishes to do spelling lists then they should operate from a paper system. Why use an expensive computer when it can be used so creatively in other ways that cannot be achieved using paper-based systems? One of the reasons dyslexic pupils enjoy ICT is that it is an area they have not previously failed in. It is important to use software in a creative, positive manner which empowers the students. In this way, the computer use does not mirror any previous experiences the students might have had when trying to learn, especially as those experiences could have been negative, representing failure and frustration.

Above all, software needs to be exciting, stimulating, enjoyable, fun and provide an engaging educational environment. No software replaces good teaching, but it can consolidate good practice. By understanding the dyslexic students and their particular strengths and difficulties, one can select software that helps and facilitates while not labelling or insulting the students. Good software is also useful for other pupils/siblings so it represents better value for money.

Summary

Chapter 11

ICT solutions for assessing/ screening dyslexia

This chapter will consider the use of ICT for identifying and screening children who might be dyslexic, or who might be at risk of dyslexia. It will be useful for both parents and teachers for, although these systems are designed to be used by suitably qualified professionals, it is important to know what is available.

The programs mentioned below are the ones that I use regularly but they are for illustration only. They serve to demonstrate the potential of using a computer for identifying and screening pupils.

Cognitive Profiling System (CoPS) (LUCID)

Children with dyslexia often 'slip through the net' for a variety of reasons. First, possibly the teacher does not appreciate the phonological and memory weaknesses of dyslexia. Secondly, some educational psychologists have been sceptical about the existence of dyslexia and some LEAs have refused to recognise the condition. Thirdly, diagnosis of Specific Learning Difficulty (dyslexia) has always been based on the principle of establishing a significant discrepancy between intelligence and literacy attainment. In general, psychologists look for evidence that literacy development is lagging behind expected levels by at least two years, which has effectively precluded the identification of dyslexia in children under the age of 7 or 8.

Screening systems for identifying children with dyslexia at an early stage of their schooling are regarded as highly desirable. Rather than label children at an early age, teachers are seeking a screening system that will identify strengths and weaknesses in cognitive abilities that are known to underpin literacy development.

The provisions of the *Code of Practice for the Identification and Assessment of Special Educational Needs* (DfEE 1994) specifically states that schools should use screening tests in order to accomplish early identification. A favourable solution for this problem lies in the ability of the computer to administer, precisely and objectively, testing materials that are sufficiently complex to yield acceptable degrees of accuracy, but in a manner that is efficient for teachers.

Computer-based tests can be much more attractive to children than conventional assessments, which might appear threatening, resulting in the children being reluctant to participate, as they do not want to be seen to fail.

Lucid CoPS (Cognitive Profiling System) is a fully computerised psychometric assessment system for use with children aged from 4 years 0 months through to 8 years 11 months. The purpose of CoPS is to identify children's cognitive strengths and weaknesses, which can give an early indication of children who are at risk of dyslexia and other learning difficulties.

CoPS consists of a range of tests and is designed to be administered in a school environment. It takes about an hour to conduct the full suite of tests in CoPS, but it is best to administer them over a period of a few weeks. The children enjoy doing these tests which are in the form of games. Any trained adult can administer CoPS, and this need not be a teacher. Teachers' aides, curriculum support assistants, an SEN governor, a dinner supervisor and helpful parents have helped me to administer CoPS.

CoPS consists of eight tests which are listed in Table 11.1.

Table 11.1 CoPS tests

Name of test	Principal cognitive mode	Principal processing skills being assessed
Zoid's Friends	Visual	Sequential memory (colours)
Rabbits	Visual	Sequential memory (spatial + temporal)
Toybox	Visual	Associative memory (shape + colour)
Zoid's Letters	Visual	Sequential memory (symbols)
Zoid's Letter Names	Auditory/verbal	Associative memory (symbols + names)
Races	Auditory/verbal	Sequential memory (names)
Rhymes	Auditory/verbal	Phonological awareness (rhyming)
Wock	Auditory/verbal	Auditory discrimination
Clown	Visual	Colour discrimination (supplementary test)

When the suite of tests is completed, the information generated by CoPS is valuable in enabling the teacher to recognise the learning styles of all children in the age range. This can assist the teacher to differentiate teaching so that it addresses individual educational needs more appropriately.

Programs such CoPS should ideally be used for screening all children on school entry, or as soon as is convenient. When used in this way, it can reveal many children who are likely to encounter significant difficulties in developing literacy skills, but who might otherwise have gone undetected at that stage. The typical problems that would be experienced later by such children in their educational development may then be addressed swiftly and before these children have been discouraged by failure. However, CoPS can also be used for the assessment of any child within the specified age range who has encountered difficulties in learning. In such cases, CoPS can help to reveal underlying cognitive causes of learning difficulties such as weak auditory discrimination.

CoPS is designed to be used by teachers, psychologists and other appropriately trained and qualified persons working in education or related professions.

Although CoPS is straightforward to administer, interpretation of the results requires expertise in education and/or psychology, and so it is not designed for use by parents or untrained personnel. The CoPS tests yield a graphical profile of the child's cognitive strengths and weaknesses, based on standardised norms. The graphical profile may be printed out, if desired, and used in consultation with psychologists and other educational specialists in formulating an individual learning programme. Figure 11.1 gives a graphical profile of a pupil who has phonological processing difficulties.

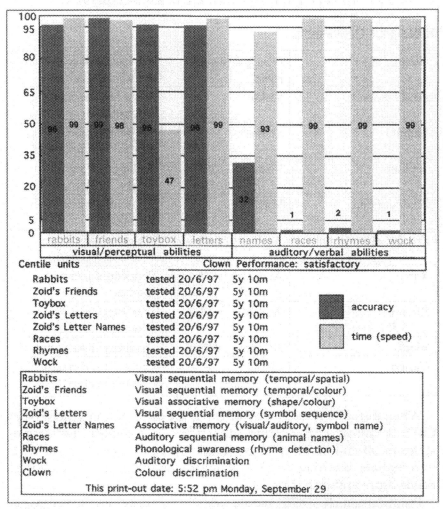

Figure 11.1 Chart showing child's performance relative to population

After interpreting the CoPS results and making recommendations for educational action, two fundamental educational strategies need to be borne in mind: educational strategies to ameliorate cognitive weaknesses; and differentiated teaching in literacy. These two approaches should complement each other. Many of the cognitive abilities that are especially important for early literacy generally improve with practice. Where CoPS reveals limitation in these skills, the teacher knows where, and with which students, to give help.

However, the objective of CoPS is not to just identify specific cognitive weaknesses so that these can be given training. An equally important function of CoPS is to give the teacher insights into the child's pattern of cognitive strengths and weaknesses. This enables the teacher to make the literacy learning programme for the child more individual. Thus the best overall approach is usually one which attempts to remedy weaknesses while at the same time builds on strengths. Many dyslexic children have strengths in visual memory, which can be utilised in developing alternative strategies for learning.

CoPS Baseline

Baseline Assessment refers to any method of evaluating children's abilities and level of development when they first enter school. In September 1996 the Secretary of State for Education and Employment announced government proposals for a National Framework for Baseline Assessment. Since September 1998, schools in England and Wales have been required to assess all children on entry using a baseline assessment scheme which conforms to the National Framework monitored by the Qualifications and Curriculum Authority (QCA).

CoPS Baseline Assessment is a computer-assisted baseline assessment instrument for evaluating children's abilities and levels of development when they first enter schools and has been accredited by the QCA. CoPS Baseline gives the teacher an instant profile of each new entrant. This profile establishes levels and ranges of ability, identifying strengths and limitations. The tests are quick to administer, with the teacher only having to spend about 20 minutes with each child individually. CoPS Baseline is suitable for all children in the age range 4 years 0 months to 5 years 6 months.

The **Communications** module assesses the fundamental expressive language abilities required for good communication and learning, including vocabulary knowledge, maturity of grammar and phonology, fluency of expression and accuracy of description.

The **Literacy** module assesses the receptive language abilities that form the basis of effective literacy development, including verbal comprehension, awareness of print, letter recognition, phonological skills and basic reading and spelling.

The **Mathematics** module assesses the concepts and skills that young children need for mathematics learning, including grasp of fundamental mathematical language, recognition of shape and pattern, understanding of classification, seriation and original position, basic number recognition, and simple addition and subtraction.

The **Personal and Social Development** sections include maturity of social and emotional behaviour, the child's relationship with peers and adults, concentration and attention, motivation for learning, motor skills and coordination.

CoPS Baseline produces Teacher Reports, which give all the numerical results, and Parent Reports. The latter summarise the child's performance in each module and give a brief explanation of the assessment.

Brief recommendations for teaching intended as guidelines only are included in the reports.

Despite an increase in awareness of dyslexia over recent years there are still a surprising number of children who are not identified in primary education. Of those who are identified, most are at least 7–8 years old and are, therefore, likely to have experienced two or three years of constant failure in the school environment. These children may lose the motivation to learn and may become disruptive. Consequently, it is of great importance that dyslexia is identified as early as possible to prevent children from losing their self-confidence.

LASS (Lucid)

For older pupils from Y3 onwards, Lucid Assessment Systems for Schools (LASS) is available. These are fully computerised multifunctional assessment systems for use with students. Junior LASS is for age ranges 7 years 0 months to 10 years 11 months and Secondary LASS is for students in the age range 11 years 0 months to 15 years 11 months. The tests are standardised, so that teachers using the system will be able to establish where any given student fell on any of the components of the suite, in relation to the population norms.

Using LASS, it is easy to spot students who are under-performing in literacy in relation to their age and/or intellectual potential. It is also straightforward to verify if any difficulties are likely to be of a dyslexic nature. All this information can be used in the formulation of schemes of work and Individual Education Plans (IEPs) and is valuable when deliberating whether or not to request a formal assessment by an educational psychologist.

Many junior and secondary schools assess the abilities of new entrants in verbal and non-verbal abilities, literacy attainment and reasoning skills. LASS can fulfil several of these functions, including the non-verbal ability and literacy attainment components. LASS also provides schools with a straightforward screening system for special educational needs, which can be an adjunct to routine testing and profiling. Alternatively either system can be used at any time between the ages of 7–11/11–15. When used for this purpose, students who have a low score in any of the routine profiling modules (Reasoning, Single Word Reading, Sentence Reading and Spelling), or who display a significant discrepancy between the score on Reasoning and the score(s) on Single Word Reading or Spelling, would automatically be administered the diagnostic modules.

The eight tests in LASS are listed in Table 11.2.

The **Reasoning** module gives an estimate of the child's general intelligence. This is a matrix test, in which both visual and verbal reasoning strategies may be employed. There is good evidence that such matrix reasoning tests provide a good overall indicator of general intellectual ability.

Table 11.2 LASS tests

Name of test	Description
Cave	A test of visual memory for objects and spatial positions
Mobile	An auditory memory test assessing digit span
Non-word Reading	A test of phonic decoding skills
Syllable Segmentation	A test of syllable and phoneme deletion that identifies poor phonological processing ability
Single Word Reading	A test that involves selecting a single word from five options
Sentence Reading	An adaptive test that involves finding the missing words in sentences
Spelling	An adaptive test that involves spelling single words
Reasoning	An adaptive test involving matrix puzzles that can be solved by a careful application of logical reasoning, using both visual and verbal strategies

Sentence Reading involves both reading accuracy and reading comprehension. Hence it gives a good general estimate of the overall reading skills of students in this age range.

Single Word Reading is a 20-item test of word recognition out-of-context (reading accuracy).

Non-words are letter strings that are not recognised words, but conform to orthographic rules of the language. For example, 'gade' or 'tiphalune' are not English words but are nevertheless pronounceable as though they were words, using phonological decoding skills. Dyslexic students typically experience difficulties in reading non-words.

Segments is a test of general phonological processing abilities requiring deletion of segments of words. For example, 'butterfly' without the syllable 'ter' would be pronounced 'buh'fly'. There is good evidence that dyslexic individuals of all ages have persistent difficulties with this type of task.

Spelling: poor spelling often signals deeper cognitive difficulties, e.g. in memory, that can create problems in many aspects of education. However, poor spelling does not inevitably indicate dyslexia. If there are no underlying cognitive difficulties, it is usually the case that they have never been taught to spell properly, or have had insufficient practice in using their spelling skills so that these skills become automatised.

Cave is a test of visual memory, involving spatial and temporal sequences. In cases of literacy difficulties it is important for the teacher to know whether the student's visual memory skills are weak or strong as these will have implications for subsequent teaching recommendations.

Mobile is a test of auditory-verbal sequential memory, based on recall of digits. It is a well-established fact that individuals with dyslexia or Specific Learning Difficulty typically experience problems with recall of digits.

I was presented recently with a pupil who I felt was manipulating the paper-based tests I was using to assess his auditory memory. I placed him on the appropriate section in LASS, which was the Mobile test, and I asked him if he would like to play a game on the computer where he could order pizzas for the hungry character on the screen. **He was totally unaware that he was being assessed and enjoyed the activity immensely.** The result was that he managed to demonstrate his excellent auditory memory and the computer registered the data, presenting it in a graphical format.

Summary

Computerised assessments have been shown to have a number of advantages over conventional pen-and-paper tests. They are less threatening, as children may not be aware that they are being tested. Test administration using a computer is more objective and precise than conventional tests that can be administered differently by different people. Computerised tests are also labour-saving, as there is little training needed to use them and scores are calculated automatically.

Chapter 12

Conclusion

The objective of this book has been to demonstrate that ICT is powerful and, with appropriate use, can make life easier for dyslexic pupils. ICT helps dyslexic pupils to access NC subjects and, by doing so, the pupils achieve nearer their potential, resulting in increased self-confidence and esteem. This, in turn, reduces stress, not just for the dyslexic pupils themselves, but for those involved in working with them.

Computers can represent a challenging, or even threatening environment for adults. ICT is often an area where what is possible to support and facilitate dyslexic students, along with what can be achieved, is not often realised. I hope that some fears of using ICT have been allayed, while its potential has been recognised.

ICT need not be expensive. Low-tech ICT solutions, e.g. the use of cassette recorders, can be sufficient to provide access to some subjects for dyslexic students. It is important to determine what type of ICT support provides the best solution.

When contemplating purchasing computers it is one of those rare occasions when the ends dictate the means. One must consider what software is required and then use a computer with the necessary specification to run that software. Parents and teachers need to look at what is needed and avoid transient trends, while bearing in mind that money is not the answer to everything and neither is high technology.

Purchasing computer equipment requires one to consider maintenance factors and after-sales support. Firms offering good after-sales care can prove their worth when anything goes wrong.

When using software it is important to start with programs that are relatively easy to use, enjoyable and entertaining. As confidence grows, further ICT skills will be acquired, which will enable the natural progression to using more complex software. Enhanced ICT skills will enable the writing process to be supported. This is an area most dyslexics have a problem with, and so supporting it is a principle aim.

Word-processors are an excellent tool in their own right and they can be creatively adapted to become a very effective means of support for dyslexic students. Equally, by sensibly selecting a complementary package, which adds further assistance, even greater results can be achieved.

In my opinion, it is important that industry standard software, such as Microsoft Office, with access to the web and email, is used with dyslexic pupils. This type of software gives the students the added advantage that they are already familiar with the software most likely to be used when they leave school. It also gives them peer equality and does not label them as different, which can always be interpreted as inadequate, stupid or just plain thick.

The practical ideas mentioned throughout the book give suggestions to support dyslexic students by using ICT in virtually every single subject and at each key stage. While doing this, ICT provides practice for the cognitive areas that are the weakest in dyslexic students, namely short-term memory, sequencing, spelling and reading, as well as eliciting their specific strengths.

Although ICT is important and useful, it does involve a learning curve for pupils, teachers and parents. However, it does not matter, in my opinion, if the pupil knows more than the parents or teachers about ICT, for this merely raises the self-confidence of the pupils. The effort involved in acquiring the ICT skills needed is well worth while, for ICT teaches life-long skills and enables pupils to achieve more of their full potential. As a result the pupils are indeed happier and more confident. ICT is not threatening, but is a supportive structure and environment. Computers become a non-critical friend for life.

Teachers will find that the pupils make much better progress and this will result in improved examination results, both for the pupils and the schools. Parents will be able to provide active support for their children in a positive way. Both teachers and parents will gain a feeling of satisfaction from seeing the dyslexic pupils making genuine progress and having greater access to the education environment.

Above all, by using ICT wisely, there is light at the end of the tunnel. Dyslexic pupils will build on what is taught in order to develop themselves further. This then opens up better employment opportunities with increased self-esteem.

I sincerely hope that the content and ideas contained within the chapters of this book serve to inspire you to use ICT in a creative way, giving support and benefit to the children who are dyslexic. Their enjoyment in using ICT, their subsequent successes academically, as well as their increased levels of self-confidence and happiness, will be ample reward for your hard work and efforts.

Useful information

British Dyslexia Association
98 London Road
Reading RG1 5AU
Tel: Helpline 0118 966 8271
Tel: Administration 0118 966 2677
Fax: 0118 935 1927
Email: admin@bda-
dyslexia.demon.co.uk
Web: http://www.bda-
dyslexia.org.uk/

The National Curriculum
The Stationery Office
The Publications Centre
PO Box 29
St Crispins House
Dulce Street
Norwich
NR3 1GN
Tel: 0870 600 5522

BETT Exhibition
Olympia, London
Dates: usually the first 2–3
weeks in January
Tel: 01925 241642

Colin Redman
SEN Marketing
Dyslexia Bookshop
618 Leeds Road, Outwood
Wakefield WF1 2LT
Tel/fax: 01924 871697
Email:
sen.marketing@ukonline.co.uk

Software suppliers

ABLAC Learning Works Ltd
South Devon House
Newton Abbot
Devon TQ12 2BP
Tel: 01626 332233
Fax: 01626 331464

Crick Software Ltd
35 Charter Gate
Quary Park Close
Moulton Park
Northampton NN3 6QB
Tel: 01604 671691
Fax: 01604 671692
Web: www.cricksoft.com

Don Johnston Special Needs Ltd
18 Clarendon Court
Calver Road
Winwick Quay
Warrington WA2 8QP
Tel: 01925 241642
Fax 01925 241745

Fisher Marriott
Fax: 024 76616325

iANSYS
The White House
72 Fen Road
Cambridge CB4 1UN
Tel: 01223 420101
Fax: 01223 426644
Email: sales@dyslexia.com

LUCID
PO BOX 63
Beverley
East Yorkshire HU17 8ZZ
Tel/fax: 01482 465589

Peter Wilkes
Better Books & Software
3 Paganel Drive
Dudley
West Midlands
DY1 4AZ

REM
Great Western House
Langport
Somerset TA10 9YU
Tel: 01458 253636
Fax: 01458 254701
Web: http://www.r-e-m.co.uk

Sherston Software Ltd
Angel House
High Street, Sherston
SN16 0WY
Tel: 01666 843200
Fax: 01666 843216

TAG Developments Ltd
Dept PR102
FREEPOST
SEA 1562
25 Pelham Road
Gravesend
Kent DA11 0BR
Tel: 0800 591262
Fax: 01474 537887
Email: sales@tagdev.co.uk

SCET
74 Victoria Crescent Road
Glasgow G12 9JN
Tel: 0141 337 5000
Fax: 0141 337 5050

TextHELP Systems Ltd
Enkalon Business Centre
25 Randalstown Road
Antrim BT41 4IJ
Tel: 02894 428105
Fax: 02894 428574
Web: www.texthelp.com

Valiant Technology Ltd
3 Grange Mills
Weir Road
London SW12 0NE
Tel: 020 8673 2233
Fax: 020 8673 6333

White Space Ltd
41 Mall Road
London W6 9DG
Tel/fax: 020 8748 5927
Email:
wordshark@btinternet.com

Bibliography

Department for Education (DfEE) (1994) *Code of Practice for the Identification and Assessment of Special Educational Needs.* London: HMSO.

HMSO (1978) *Special Educational Needs Report of the Committee of Enquiry into the Education of Handicapped Children and Young People,* May 1978. London: HMSO.

Horne, J. K. *et al.* (1999) *Lucid Assessment System for Schools.* Lucid Creative Ltd, East Yorkshire.

Nicolson, R. I. *et al.* (1995) 'Dyslexia, articulation and the cerebellum'. Paper presented at the 47th Annual Conference of the Orton Dyslexia Society, Boston, USA.

School Curriculum Assessment Authority (SCAA) (1995) *Early Intervention in Children with Reading Difficulties.* Discussion Paper No 2, February.

School Curriculum Assessment Authority (SCAA) (1997) *The National Framework for Baseline Assessment: Criteria and Procedures for Accreditation of Baseline Assessment Schemes.* London: School Curriculum and Assessment Authority.

Thomas, K. V. *et al.* (1997) 'Computer-based identification of dyslexia and special educational needs'. Paper presented at the 25th Anniversary Conference of the British Dyslexia Association, University of York.

Index